CGFM

Examination 1: Governmental Environment

SECRETS

Study Guide
Your Key to Exam Success

CGFM Exam Review for the Certified
Government Financial Manager Exam

Dear Future Exam Success Story:

Congratulations on your purchase of our study guide. Our goal in writing our study guide was to cover the content on the test, as well as provide insight into typical test taking mistakes and how to overcome them.

Standardized tests are a key component of being successful, which only increases the importance of doing well in the high-pressure high-stakes environment of test day. How well you do on this test will have a significant impact on your future, and we have the research and practical advice to help you execute on test day.

The product you're reading now is designed to exploit weaknesses in the test itself, and help you avoid the most common errors test takers frequently make.

How to use this study guide

We don't want to waste your time. Our study guide is fast-paced and fluff-free. We suggest going through it a number of times, as repetition is an important part of learning new information and concepts.

First, read through the study guide completely to get a feel for the content and organization. Read the general success strategies first, and then proceed to the content sections. Each tip has been carefully selected for its effectiveness.

Second, read through the study guide again, and take notes in the margins and highlight those sections where you may have a particular weakness.

Finally, bring the manual with you on test day and study it before the exam begins.

Your success is our success

We would be delighted to hear about your success. Send us an email and tell us your story. Thanks for your business and we wish you continued success.

Sincerely,

Mometrix Test Preparation Team

Need more help? Check out our flashcards at: <u>http://MometrixFlashcards.com/CGFM</u>

TABLE OF CONTENTS

Top 20 Test Taking Tips

1. Carefully follow all the test registration procedures
2. Know the test directions, duration, topics, question types, how many questions
3. Setup a flexible study schedule at least 3-4 weeks before test day
4. Study during the time of day you are most alert, relaxed, and stress free
5. Maximize your learning style; visual learner use visual study aids, auditory learner use auditory study aids
6. Focus on your weakest knowledge base
7. Find a study partner to review with and help clarify questions
8. Practice, practice, practice
9. Get a good night's sleep; don't try to cram the night before the test
10. Eat a well balanced meal
11. Know the exact physical location of the testing site; drive the route to the site prior to test day
12. Bring a set of ear plugs; the testing center could be noisy
13. Wear comfortable, loose fitting, layered clothing to the testing center; prepare for it to be either cold or hot during the test
14. Bring at least 2 current forms of ID to the testing center
15. Arrive to the test early; be prepared to wait and be patient
16. Eliminate the obviously wrong answer choices, then guess the first remaining choice
17. Pace yourself; don't rush, but keep working and move on if you get stuck
18. Maintain a positive attitude even if the test is going poorly
19. Keep your first answer unless you are positive it is wrong
20. Check your work, don't make a careless mistake

Organization and structure of Government

Levels of government

Federal: The federal government is a representative democratic republic. It is charged with creating, administering, and interpreting the laws of the country as a whole. The U.S. government is federal because each of these three roles is divided among separate branches of government. The officials of the U.S. government are chosen by its citizens in free elections. Additionally, the federal government is charged with protecting the nation and its interests.

State: The state government oversees matters that lie entirely within its borders. These matters include working conditions, state criminal code, business conduct, utilities, etc. A state's power to enact its own laws is limited by the federal government which requires that no state laws violate the U.S. Constitution or the laws or treaties of the federal government.

Local: The types and organization of city governments varies widely across the U.S. Local governments are typically more directly involved in providing services and resources to its citizens than the other two levels of government. Local governments generally oversee police and fire protection, health and sanitary codes, education, public transportation, and housing matters. Most local governments utilize some form of central counsel and a head executive, who are elected by voting citizens, to manage the affairs of the locality.

Integration
Integration is considered vital to the proper functioning of the U.S. government. The national government is policy driven and furthest removed from affected citizens. Therefore, state and local governments are necessary to implement the national government's policies in the most effective way for its citizens. Integration is so important that it even extends from government to private non-profit and for-profit entities. For example, the Salvation Army is a non-profit organization that helps further the government policies of job training, food provision, and housing for those in need. The national government may provide funding directly as well as indirectly (through exemption from taxation) to this organization to enable it to best achieve its purpose.

Remember that the separation of powers doctrine applies between branches of government at the same level in order to allow each branch to carry out its responsibilities while checking the actions of and being checked by the other branches. This doctrine does nothing to dissuade integration between different levels of government.

Branches of government

<u>Legislative</u>
Article I of the U.S. Constitution establishes the legislative branch of the national government. This article specifically grants all of the legislative powers of the national government to a bicameral Congress. The two components of the Congress are the Senate and the House of Representatives. Members of both the Senate and the House of Representatives are elected directly by citizens. Article I, Section 8 specifically lists the powers granted to the legislative branch (there are dozens). Some of the most notable of these powers are; to lay and collect taxes, to borrow money on the credit of the United States, to regulate commerce, to declare war, etc.

<u>Executive</u>
Article II of the U.S. Constitution outlines both the role and the power of the executive branch of the national government. The power of the executive branch is vested in the President, who also serves as Commander in Chief of the Armed Forces. The President appoints the Cabinet and oversees the various components of the executive branch (various agencies and departments). Additionally, Article II vests in the President the authority to grant pardons and reprieves for offenses against the United States (except for cases involving impeachment) and to make treaties with other countries (with 2/3 approval from the Senate). Furthermore, the President may nominate (with the consent and approval of the Senate) U.S. Supreme Court Justices, ambassadors, and all other officers of the U.S. government. Article II, Section 1 specifically sets forth the oath that a President must take before entering office. This oath is as follows: "I do solemnly swear (or affirm) that I will faithfully execute the office of President of the United States, and will to the best of my ability, preserve, protect and defend the Constitution of the United States."

<u>Judicial</u>
The judicial branch of the national government is established by Article III of the U.S. Constitution. Article III, Section 1 states that judicial power is vested into one Supreme Court and any inferior courts as the legislative branch may create. The justices of national courts hold their offices until such time as they retire. The power of the judicial branch "extends to all cases, in law or equity arising under this Constitution, the laws of the United States, and treaties made, or which shall be made, under their authority;--to all cases affecting ambassadors, other public ministers and consuls;--to all cases of admiralty and maritime jurisdiction;--to controversies to which the United States shall be a party;--to controversies between two or more states;--between a state and citizens of another state;--between citizens of different states;--between citizens of the same state claiming lands under grants of different states, and between a state, or the citizens thereof, and foreign states, citizens or subjects."

<u>Establishing the branches</u>
The branches of the national government are established specifically by the U.S. Constitution. Recall that because of the Reservation Clause of the U.S. Constitution,

the national government is empowered only to the extent specifically enumerated in the U.S. Constitution. The U.S. Constitution specifically dictates that the three branches of the national government shall be separate but equal. The U.S. Constitution ensured this equality by granting each branch both shared and individual powers. Similarly, the branches of all state governments are established by the constitution for that particular state. Note that each state's constitution differs from the others. As a result, different names (particularly for the legislative branch) are often used.

Components

Very generally, the various components of the three branches of the national government exist to help each branch perform its designated functions. For example, one component of the judicial branch is the U.S. Court of Appeals. These courts hear cases that are appealed from lower federal courts, enabling the U.S. Supreme Court to focus more on adjudicating the constitutional validity of laws passed by the legislative branch and other core functions. It is important to note that this works similarly at the State and local level with the components specifically tailored to the particular needs of each locality. Some of the major components of each branch include:

- Legislative: Architect of the Capitol, U.S. Botanic Garden, General Accounting Office, Government Printing Office, Library of Congress, Congressional Budget Office.
- Executive: White House Office, Office of the Vice President, Council of Economic Advisers, Council on Environment Quality, National Security Council, Office of Administration, Office of Management and Budget, Office of National Drug Control Policy, Office of Policy Development, Office of Science and Technology Policy, Office of the U.S. Trade Representative, and the Departments of Agriculture, Commerce, Defense, Education, Energy, Health and Human Services, Homeland Security, Housing and Urban Development, The Interior, Justice, Labor, State, Transportation, Treasury, and Veterans Affairs.
- Judicial: U.S. Courts of Appeals, U.S. District Courts, Territorial Courts, U.S. Court of International Trade, U.S. Court of Federal Claims, U.S. Court of Appeals for the Armed Forces, U.S. Tax Court, U.S. Court of Appeals for Veterans Claims, Administrative Office of the U.S. Courts, Federal Judicial Center, and U.S. Sentencing Commission.

Executive orders function

At both the national and the state level, the legislative branch is empowered to make laws. Outside of the veto process, the executive branch is has little to do with the legislative branch's lawmaking process. However, executive orders allow the chief executive (e.g., President or Governor) to implement policy in a manner that bypasses the legislative process. From the chief executive's perspective there are pros and cons to using executive orders. On the positive side, the chief executive has much more control over executive orders than legislation. Additionally, the process is much faster and streamlined. Also, the chief executive does not have to secure the necessary votes in Congress that are otherwise required to implement desired legislation. On the other hand, executive orders are beneath the constitution and laws in the authoritative hierarchy. As a result, executive orders cannot violate provisions of the constitution or laws. Further, any subsequent chief executive can revoke any executive order in existence.

<u>Note</u>: There is no specific law or provision in the U.S. Constitution that permits executive orders. Article II, Sections 1 and 3 come the closest with vague mentions of executive power.

Authorities

All levels of government have four types of authorities; executive orders, laws, constitutions, and rules and regulations. Their hierarchical order is as follows:
- Constitutions: At each level of government, the constitution (or the local law equivalent, Charter) is the highest legal authority. There is one constitution at the national level and each state has its own constitution. The U.S. Constitution is the supreme law of the United States. As such, all other constitutions and laws must not violate it.
- Laws: Laws are drafted by national and state legislatures. Laws may be drafted so that they are permanent or temporary in nature. When the legislature passes a law, the executive has the power to veto the law subject to Congress' overriding the veto. Passed legislation is also subject to judicial review. Unlike the veto, there is no congressional override if the Supreme Court finds that the law violates the Constitution.
- Executive Orders: These are edicts from the executive branch of government (the President at the national level). There is no direct authority in the U.S. Constitution granting the executive branch the power to issue executive orders. However, Article II of the U.S. Constitution does vaguely grant power to the executive branch. These orders cannot violate laws or the constitution.
- Rules and Regulations: These are drafted by various executive branch agencies. There purpose is to assist policy objectives by further explaining laws. Rules and regulations must not violate executive orders, laws, or the constitution

Municipal governments

It is important to note that the municipal governments from state to state vary widely. Municipal governments are one of two components of the typical local government. The other component is county government. All forms of local government derive their power from a Charter created by their state's government. These Charters specify the local government's structure and responsibilities. Municipal governments are typically distinguishable from state to state based on the relationship between their executive and legislative branches. For example, some states' municipalities are structured with a mayor and city council (the relative power of these two entities also varies from state to state). Other states incorporate a municipal government system whereby the executive and legislative functions are combined in the authority of the commissioners. Finally, some states adopt a system where there is a council and a manager. It is interesting to note that the manager is not elected by citizen vote, but rather chosen by the council. Note that municipalities often have municipal courts that make up a judicial branch.

Government commissions

Government commissions are another component of government. There are two types of government commissions, permanent and temporary. Permanent commissions are created to fulfill a regulatory role where there is an ongoing need. Temporary commissions are formed to work on a particular issue or complete a specific study. All three branches of the U.S. government have commissions. Additionally, commissions exist at all three levels (national, state, and local) of government. The law creating it dictates the structure of a particular commission.

Generally, in the case of executive commissions at the national level, the President selects members of executive commissions (with Congressional consent). At the state and local level, commissioners may be appointed by the chief executive or directly elected by the citizens of that jurisdiction.

Examples of government commissions include historic district commissions (local level), environmental commissions (state level), and the Tower Commission (national level-presidential).

Governmental authority

Starting at the national level, the U.S. Constitution grants the national government specific powers. All powers not specifically granted to the national government are retained by the states. This is accomplished through the Tenth Amendment to the U.S. Constitution (also referred to as the Reserve Clause). States draft their own constitutions. State constitutions determine how local governments are created and organized. Local governments typically have charters. These charters are the highest law at the local level and act as the local government's constitution.

The U.S. Constitution is supreme to all other laws and constitutions at the national or lower levels. Therefore, state constitutions (or state laws) may not violate the constitution or laws of the United States. Local charters and laws, similarly, cannot violate their state's constitution or laws, or the constitution or laws of the United States. The United States Supreme Court has final authority on determining whether or not a state's constitutional provision (or state or local law) violates the U.S. Constitution.

10th Amendment

The 10th Amendment to the U.S. Constitution reads:
> The powers not delegated to the United States by the Constitution, nor prohibited by it to the states, are reserved to the states respectively, or to the people.

The 10th Amendment is also referred to as the States' Rights Amendment or the Reserved Clause. The origins of the 10th Amendment suggest that its adoption was not intended to add anything new to the reading of the U.S. Constitution. Instead, it was meant to clearly state that the national government would not be able to exercise powers that were beyond those specifically granted to it or that states would lose their reserved powers. It should be noted that this does not mean that the national government doesn't have methods by which it can greatly influence lower levels of government.

Government entities

General-Purpose: These types of government entities are very broad in scope. They oversee several areas of policy. General-purpose government entities exist at the national, state, and local level.

Local general-purpose: Governments generate revenue from imposing taxes (income, property, and/or sales), collecting user fees, and obtaining aid from national or state governments.

Special-Purpose: These types of government entities are very narrow in scope. Special-purpose government entities exist to administer a very specific role of government. An example of a special-purpose government entity is the York Rural Sanitary District. General-purpose government entities create special-purpose government entities via power derived from their constitutions, laws, or charters (recall that charters are local government's equivalent to a constitution). In addition to being created by a general-purpose government entity, special-purpose government entities may be formed in response to the passing of a local ordinance calling for their creation or in response to a successful ballot initiative. Funding for special-purpose government entities typically flows down from the general-purpose government entity that the special-purpose government entity is affiliated with. However, some special-purpose government entities are enabled to impose taxes, charge user fees, or assume debt in order to fund their operations.

Number of government entities
At the national and state level, the number of general-purpose government entities has been static for a long time (one national general-purpose government entity, fifty state general-purpose government entities). Additionally, while new local general-purpose entities emerge and disappear, this number has been fairly constant over the last several years. However, special-purpose government entities,

especially at the local level, greatly fluctuate in number (with substantial growth recently in the number of special-purpose, non-school, government entities).

General-purpose county governments

Generally speaking, there are three types of general-purpose government entities at the local level. These are county, municipality, and township government. Most states utilize county governments (Louisiana and Alaska use different nomenclature, but function similarly to other states). States form county governments under the authority of their state constitution or laws. Typically, states are geographically subdivided into counties (or boroughs or parishes), which encompass municipalities and townships. However, some major cities are not included within any county of the state. Citizens of these cities are, therefore, not served by any county government. In jurisdictions where cities (even major ones) are included within counties, the county government and city government will divide responsibilities. Some large counties elect an executive (similar to a mayor at the municipal lever or governor at the state level) in addition to an elected supervisory board. More often, the citizens of the county elect supervisors to a board. This board, in turn, appoints a county administrator and various other officials. Members of the supervisory board may be elected based on geographic location within the county, at large, or both. Again, the state's constitution or laws would determine this.

General-purpose municipality governments

General-purpose municipality governments typically encompass cities, towns, boroughs, and villages. Defining a municipality is difficult because they can be difficult to identify. Generically speaking, a general-purpose municipal government entity is created to govern a specific concentration of people. As population groups relocate, grow, or shrink, so will their municipal government. For example, a rural area may find itself governed only by a general-purpose county government. As this area grows in population, a general-purpose municipality government entity is formed. If the area were to continue to grow such that the needs of the citizens were not being adequately met by the existing general-purpose governments in place, additionally general-purpose municipalities could form.

Forms

States differ as to the formation and operation of general-purpose municipal government entities. The two most common forms of general-purpose municipal government entities are distinguished by identifying where their power rests. In a municipality where a council-manager structure exists, the citizens elect officials to a council. These elected officials then appoint a manager. In this construct, the elected council officials make the decisions with respect to the municipality's operations. The manager exists to undertake the actions necessary to implement the council's decisions. The council will typically appoint someone on the council to hold the title of mayor. This mayor is viewed as first among equals on the council, but has no independent legislative power.

In a municipality where a <u>mayor-council</u> structure exists, citizens elect a mayor (in addition to council members). The mayor is imbued with the authority to make decisions regarding the operations of the municipality. Additionally, the mayor may delegate operational duties to officials that he or she appoints. Keep in mind that mayors in different municipalities possess different levels of power. These different levels of power often delineate different municipalities as either a strong mayor or weak mayor system.

<u>General–purpose township governments</u>
During the early days of the United States, all land was carved into six mile by six mile squares. These squares were called townships. Today, many existing townships can trace their origins to this historical subdivision. But, keep in mind that less than half (twenty) of the states have government at the township level. The services provide by general-purpose township government entities are often very similar to the services provided by general-purpose municipal government entities. As a result, there can be a large amount of overlap, from a functional standpoint, between general-purpose township government entities and general-purpose municipal government entities. The level of overlap varies greatly from state to state. In some states every citizen is included in a general-purpose township government entity. While in other states, townships and municipalities are totally separated so that no citizen is governed by both a general-purpose township government entity and a general-purpose municipal government entity simultaneously.

The typical general-purpose township government entity consists of a board of elected officials, usually referred to as supervisors or trustees, and a clerk. Typical officers include justice of the peace, road commissioner, assessor, constable, and surveyors.

Quasi-governmental entities

In addition to general-purpose and special-purpose government entities, there are quasi-governmental entities. These entities are hybrids in that they possess legal characteristics of both government and private sector entities. Quasi-government entities typically:
- have close association with a government agency, but are not considered part of that agency;
- are created by a government agency but not subject to the legal and administrative requirements imposed on the government agency; or
- are not created by a government agency but perform a public function and are financially subsidized by a government agency.

Quasi-government entities are often delineated by their nature and level of connection they have to an actual government agency.

Special-purpose school districts

Generally speaking, there are two types of special-purpose government entities at the local level. These are school districts and other districts. School districts are categorized as either independent or dependent. An independent school district is subject to state law only (as opposed to any lower level local government). As such, independent school districts have great latitude in their operations. For example, independent school districts can establish their own hiring and personnel review policies (subject to state/national constitution and law). Also, independent school districts are empowered to raise and assess taxes as well as issue debt instruments (typically bonds) to raise necessary operating revenue. A dependent school district, on the other hand, is governed by some other government entity. Therefore, the operations of a dependent school district are subject to the rules of some local government entity (remember, these rules cannot violate national or state constitution or law). School districts govern not only kindergarten through high school, but also some institutions of higher education (primarily junior colleges). The typical school district governing body consists of a board of elected members who appoint a superintendent. This structure applies to both independent and dependent school districts. While narrower in scope, school districts are generally equal to a city or county from an authoritative standpoint. Therefore, school districts often have similar powers (e.g., power to tax and utilize imminent domain). Note: The majority of school districts are independent.

Special-purpose districts

Special-purpose district government entities are established by a general-purpose government entity. Where general-purpose government entities must undertake many (and often competing) rules, special-purpose districts are formed to address a very specific need. Examples of special-purpose districts include: airport districts, hospital districts, levee districts, community service districts, municipal utility districts, public utility districts, parks and recreation districts, sanitary districts, water districts, resource conservation districts, and water storage districts. Special-purpose districts retain the power to establish their own administrative methods and sometimes to levy and assess taxes and issue debt instruments (typically bonds) to raise revenue. Special-purpose districts vary greatly in regards to their structure. Elected officials, appointed officials, or both, may head these entities. The most attractive aspect of creating special-purpose district government entities from a governance perspective is their flexibility. For instance, because of their narrow focus, they can be formed to oversee one specific issue as opposed to overseeing a myriad of civic needs. Also, many of these districts can fund themselves and operate in a manner that best suits their narrow responsibility rather than being subject to the same obstacles that general-purpose government entities are subjected to. Note: Many (but not all) entities that are referred to as "authorities," are actually special-purpose districts (e.g., housing authorities).

Government corporations

Government corporations are a sub-category of quasi-government entities. Government corporations typically are one hundred percent self-funded. That means that their entire operating budget comes from fees charged and revenues derived from the activity they perform. This remains true even in the case of government corporations that are granted authority to issue debt instruments because repayment of those instruments is expected to come from the government corporation's private revenue, rather than from public sources.

A benefit of government corporations from a governance standpoint is that they are subject to far less administrative regulation than government agencies and are self-funded. Government corporations exist at the national and state level. Examples include Fannie Mae, and the National Park Foundation.

It should be noted that the increasing number of special-purpose and quasi-governmental entities could lead to fragmentation and/or redundancy in the provision of government services. Additionally, the use of quasi-government entities is controversial because some feel it places additional layers between citizens elected officials, therefore diluting the influence of voting power.

Federalism

Black's Law Dictionary defines federalism as "the legal relationship and distribution of power between the national and regional governments within a federal system of government" (8th ed. 2004). It is important to note that while most people use the term "Federalism" or "Federal" to describe the national government, it is actually a descriptive term that broadly outlines the structure of the U.S. government and the interrelation between its various levels.

Hierarchy of the state government

In the Tenth Amendment of the US Constitution, some powers are reserved for the states. All states have a hierarchy that is modeled after the federal government in that they have three branches:
1. Executive: These are the elected officials including the governor, the attorney general, the secretary of state, auditors, and commissioners.
2. Legislative: This branch is made up of elected representatives that represent the state in all legislative matters. US Senators pass laws at the federal level, while state senators consider items that will be brought forward to the governor. These representatives also are responsible for approving the state's budget and tax laws.
3. Judicial: This branch is led by the state supreme court. Generally, cases are heard at a lower-level state court, and appeals can be made to the state supreme court.

Hierarchy of local government

The local government is generally divided into two different tiers:
1. Counties and Boroughs: Each state is divided into counties or boroughs. The county lines shift from time to time as maps are redrawn. The county or borough in which someone lives determines things like real estate taxes, and school district assignments. Each county has its own governmental complex including a court house that hears local cases. Counties also maintain the libraries and have several elected commissioners that form the County Commission and the Board of Education.
2. Cities/towns/municipalities (different terms are used in different parts of the country). Generally, each city is responsible for maintaining city parks, and running police and fire departments. Most cities are run by a mayor and a city council, all of which are elected as part of local elections.

Legal and other environmental aspects of Government

Sovereignty

Black's Law Dictionary defines sovereignty as "supreme dominion, authority, or rule" (8th ed. 2004). The national government of the U.S. is said to be sovereign because it is only liable to lawsuits brought by its states and citizens to the extent it so permits. However, the sovereignty of the U.S. national government is somewhat limited. Because the U.S. national government is comprised of officials and representatives elected by its citizens, it is these citizens that truly hold the sovereignty. This citizen-held sovereignty is known as "popular sovereignty."

To establish a framework, the concept of sovereignty is relative to the entity being discussed. Therefore, the U.S. national government is sovereign, yet the ultimate power rests in the hands of the citizens. Similarly, state governments are sovereign in that they possess powers that are independent of the national government; however, the states cannot enact laws directly contradicting those laws or the constitution of the national government. Finally, local governments are also sovereign to the extent that they hold powers apart from their states; however, localities may not adopt laws which contradict the laws or constitutions of its national or state government.

Sovereignty is the exclusive right to exercise supreme political authority. In the United States, government sovereignty exists in a modified form. This form of United States government sovereignty is known as popular sovereignty. Popular sovereignty is a diluted form of sovereignty in that the people possess overall authority over government. This citizen held power is the ability to elect officials by vote. Governments obtain their sovereignty through constitutions (national and state) and charters (local). Amongst levels of government, the national government has the most extensive sovereignty, followed by state governments, and then local governments. In order to fund their operations, United States can:

- print money (national government only);
- levy and assess taxes on individuals and legal entities (e.g., income, property, and transactions);
- incur debt (typically through issuance of bonds); and
- form budgets.

Legal limitations

Recall that sovereignty in the United States is subject to the highest form of limitation, the citizen's right to vote (popular sovereignty). Additionally, various legal limitations apply to curtail the power of governments in the United States. These legal limitations originate from constitutions, statutes, and local ordinances. For example, legal limitations dictate how a government can assess and collect taxes. This is seen in the process of giving notice that taxes are due as well as the restraints placed on how governments can obtain revenues from a non-compliant tax debtor.

Legal limitations also apply to other methods used by governments to fund their operations. At the national level borrowing limitations are statutory rather than constitutional. State level borrowing restrictions come from both statutes and constitutions.

Doctrines of power

The Separation of Powers Doctrine and the Checks and Balances Doctrine serve to limit the power of each branch of government. These doctrines are in place to prevent any one branch of government from achieving an imbalance of power. This goal is achieved in two ways. First, each branch of government is assigned particular, limited powers. Second, each branch has powers over the other two branches. This is best seen through examples.

Example 1:
- Congress may pass laws.
- President may veto laws passed by Congress.

Example 2:
- President may veto laws passed by Congress.
- Congress may override the veto by a 2/3 vote.

Example 3:
- Congress may pass a law, President signs the law.
- Supreme Court determines the law to be unconstitutional.

The doctrines of separation of powers and checks and balances are contradicting notions that work to both empower and restrict the three branches of government. Under separation of powers, each branch operates independently of the others. However, there are built in checks and balances to prevent concentrations of power in any one branch and to protect the rights and liberties of citizens. Perhaps the clearest example of this is the lawmaking process. When a bill is approved by Congress to become a law, the President has the option to veto the bill preventing it from becoming law. This is an example of separation of powers in that the legislative branch is the only branch that can create law, however, that power is checked by the executive branch's ability to veto an approved bill. Interestingly, the executive branch's veto power is also checked. Following a veto, a bill returns to Congress. If the Congress vote to approve the vetoed bill by at least 2/3 (both Houses), then the bill overrides the President's veto to become law. An additional example of checks and balances on the legislative branch's ability to create laws is judicial review. The judicial branch has the power to rule a law invalid if it conflicts with the U.S. Constitution. Note that slight structural variances may exist, but state governments operate the same way.

Grants

Grants are monetary awards issued by a level of government to a lower level of government. Influence becomes a factor because the issuing level of government can dictate the terms that must be met by the lower level of government to acquire the funds available via the grant. This frequently manifests itself by the higher level of government dictating how the grant funds must be spent. Typically, grants are issued to lower levels of government for the purpose of carrying some need within the community. For example, building and maintain streets, updating utilities, education, etc. The grant system is beneficial to both the higher and lower level of government involved. The higher level of government gets some control over how its money is spent and is reassured that vital projects are undertaken at a more local level. The lower level of government receives money to complete projects and is given some flexibility in how it handles the project to better serve its locality. It is important to note that the award of grant money does not conclude the process. At all stages throughout the completion of projects funded by grant money, detailed reporting and accounting filings must be made to the issuing government to insure the proper use and allocation of grant funds.

Budgets

Appropriated

An appropriated budget is one which has made it through the lengthy, and often contentious, budget process and provides the legal authority to spend. Appropriation is reached in two different ways depending on the nature of the program being funded. If the program is a mandatory program (e.g., social security benefits), then no additional legislation is required to authorize spending. However, if the program is discretionary, then an additional piece of legislation (known as an appropriations bill) must be passed for the program to be funded.

Due to the contentious nature of the budgetary process, it is possible that no budget is passed. This creates obvious problems for governments from an operational standpoint. To avoid a cessation of government functions, the legislative branch may pass a continuing resolution. The continuing resolution funds critical operations of the government until a new budget is funded.

Implementing

Upon becoming a law, a budget is implemented by the executive branch. However, just because the budget has become law doesn't mean that there are no more checks and balances. The legislative branch continues an active role in carrying out the objectives of the budget. For example, the legislative branch may, from time to time, review the implementation of various budget programs to determine their effectiveness. Also, the legislative branch will often require that reports are filed detailing how budget money is being spent. Finally, the legislative branch may dictate the organizational form of entities created to implement the budget. Also, judicial review is present to make sure that implementation of the budget (as well as the provisions of the budget itself) comply with the constitution and laws of the jurisdiction.

Legislative process

In substance, budgets are laws just like statutes (ordinances at the local level). Both endure potentially lengthy processes to become law. First, statutes (bills at this stage) and budgets are introduced to the legislative branch where they are debated, amended, and eventually voted on. Upon passage by the legislative branch, budgets and bills go to the chief executive for signing into law. The chief executive may veto (Governors of forty states have line item veto power, President does not) both Congress approved budgets and bills. The legislative branch can subsequently override the chief executive's veto. Finally, budgets are subject to judicial review just like other laws. On the other hand, budgets do not exist in perpetuity like most laws. The national government passes a budget every year. States adopt a new budget either every year, or every other year.

*Keep in mind that budgets can earmark funds that will be utilized after the budget itself expires.

Purpose

All levels of government operate with funds collected from its citizens through somewhat limited means (e.g., taxes, fees, and tolls). This differs from the private sector where funds are generated from for-profit activities that are limited only by the imagination of those operating the private sector entities. As a result of this, governments must establish budgets primarily to allocate the monies collected in the most efficient and beneficial manner as to best serve the citizens they govern. Inherent in this goal is the requirement to rank the many needs that governments oversee so that revenue collected from the citizens is allocated to the greatest needs.

Government budgets originate in the executive branch and are then proposed to the legislative branch. However, the process starts much sooner than this. Formally, many citizens gather in town hall meetings and other informal venues to discuss their opinions as to where government revenue should be spent. Note that these meetings can take place with reference to all levels of government budgeting. These meetings may be organized by the executive or legislative branch or by citizens themselves. The executive branch takes this public sentiment into consideration when drafting its proposed budget. Additionally, the chief executive benefits from proposals and ideas (often competing) generated from formal proceedings within the executive branch. Often, the chief executive will retain the advice of experts outside of the executive branch as well. Once the executive branch proposes the budget to the legislative branch, Congress benefits from similar hearings and debates to form the foundation for their own deliberations as to how government resources should be allocated. Both the executive branch and legislative branch obtain feedback from their central support offices and other government entities. Once the budget is passed by the legislative branch and signed by the chief executive (of the legislative branch overrides the chief executive's veto), the budget becomes law and is subject to judicial review.

Secondary purpose

The primary purpose of a government's budget is to utilize public funds to address the community's needs in the most efficient manner possible. Additionally, the budget serves the secondary purpose of disclosing the needs and values of a particular community. These needs and values are seen in the programs established by the budget process. Furthermore, budgets expose how the government undertakes the task of addressing the community's needs. This disclosure allows citizens (and government entities) to see the process by which their government identifies community needs and how the government goes about allocating funds to address these needs. This disclosure subjects the government to additional scrutiny and further assures the proper use of public funds.

Recent trends

1) Strategic Planning: This is a formal process that comes before the budget. Strategic planning is entered into to streamline the budget process. This is accomplished by clearly identifying the specific policies and objectives of the specific budget that is set for debate. Even though strategic planning takes place before the formal budget process begins, it is still considered a part of the budget making effort.

2) Performance Evaluations: As in many areas of government operations, there is a current trend towards applying performance goals to budgets. This trend attempts to measure the success of government in efficiently utilizing public funds.

Goals

The National Advisory Council on State and Local Budgeting has established a framework of principles that outline the goals of the budget process.

- "Principle 1-Establish Broad Goals to Guide Government Decision Making." This principle is intended to lay the foundation for the budget process. The goals set provide a target that is the focus of the various policies and programs implemented by the budget. Goals are established only after thorough determinations of the needs of the specific jurisdiction are assessed. Upon determination of the current state of the community, goals are established that will facilitate the progression of the community from its current state to the desired state. Other principles work towards these goals by developing strategies and allocating funds to achieve the established goals.

- "Principle 2-Develop Approaches to Achieve Goals." The broad goal setting that is achieved under the first principle may be the requisite starting place for the budget making process, but the goals would be meaningless without development of specific plans to achieve these goals. Recall that in the goal-setting stage of principle one, the objective was to be broad in scope so as to provide a general direction for the government. Principle two, on the other hand, requires far greater specificity and detail in order to make sure the established goals are met. Additionally, criteria should be utilized to evaluate the effectiveness of the approaches taken to achieve the government's goals.

- "Principle 3-Develop a Budget with Approaches to Achieve Goals." This principle involves the combination of the first and second principles. At the earliest state, budget development should begin with consideration of the community goals established through application of the first principle. Budget options that are initially developed should contain approaches (developed through application of the second principle) that ensure meeting the identified goals. In addition, the plan developed must be realistic in that the resources necessary to achieve the community's goals are limited. Proper financial planning is necessary to balance the competing interests of attaining community improvement goals and conserving limited assets. Through the financial planning process, budget makers will better understand the true costs of achieving each specific goal and, therefore, make informed budgetary decisions.

- "Principle 4-Evaluate Performance and Make Adjustments." This principle reflects the need to not only review the performance of various programs and policies of the budget, but to clearly identify the criteria and methods by which the programs and policies are to be evaluated. Upon making his determination, the components of the budget can be judged as to their success and relevance. It is important to note that a program could be very successful as judged by the established criteria, yet the goal of that program ceases to remain relevant. This continual evaluation of performance and relevance is not only critical to the effectiveness of the current budget, but is also important for future goal setting.

Appropriation

Appropriation is a term used to describe a budget (or portion thereof) which has become law. Prior to becoming law, the appropriation is referred to as an appropriation bill. Upon passage by the legislative branch and signing by the chief executive (or veto override) the appropriation authorizes the government to actually spend the money it has been budgeted. Additionally, the language of the appropriation spells out the terms that the government must adhere to in spending the money that has been allocated. These legal limitations include limiting the scope of the spending to purposes that do not violate the constitution or laws, establishing timelines for which the money can be spent and the amount that can be spent.

Authorization

An authorization is actually a precursor to an appropriation. An authorization creates a program that will utilize resources to address some need of the community. Typically, before a program established by an authorization can spend money, an appropriation bill must be passed (thereby becoming an appropriation). However, this is not always the case. Where the program is considered mandatory (e.g., Social Security funding), an appropriation is not required before spending can commence. In the case of a mandatory program, the spending authority is contained in the authorization. Note that mandatory programs are permitted to spend funds until the program expires according to the law that created it, or until a subsequent law eliminates or reauthorizes the program. Non-mandatory or discretionary programs, on the other hand usually require appropriations every year for continued spending.

Note: The above is only true at the national level. At the state and local level the authorization is part of the appropriation.

Government budgets vs. private sector budgets

Both types of budgets are plans that dictate money expenditures, but that is where their similarities end. In the case of government budgets, there is a long process whereby the legislative branch studies and introduced (by the executive branch) budget, proposes changes, votes on, and eventually passes or rejects the budget. It is important to note that the executive branch spends considerable time and resources on creating their draft of the budget before it is ever proposed to the legislative branch. Furthermore, the judicial branch exercises judicial review over budget expenditures. Government budgets are set for one year (two years in some states), and are restrictive in how money can be utilized.

In the private sector, far less rules apply. Private sector budgets are subject to far less review and can be changed frequently to meet the goals of the private entity. Perhaps the most critical difference is that the goal of most private sector budgets is to find the most efficient ways to generate profit for the entity.

Major types of budgets

Operating budgets
Operating budgets are typically what is envisioned when the generic term, budget, is used. At the national level, operating budgets last for one year. At the state and local levels, operating budgets can last for up to two years. The operating budget is introduced by the executive branch and voted on by the legislative branch. Assuming passage by Congress and signing by the chief executive (or veto override),

the operational budget becomes law. Operational budgets allocate anticipated in-flows of revenue and out-flows of expenses for the operations of a specific government entity. An example of in-flows of revenue is found in the 2002 operating budget for Anchorage, Alaska. These include fees, fines, interest, and taxes. The same operating budget specifies the following out-flows of revenue (expenses): medical and dental costs for employees, salaries, and equipment maintenance. Keep in mind that operating budgets, due in part to their short time from, are based on revenue and cost projections. As a result, as the actual cash in-flows and out-flows are determined, adjustments are made to account for any shortfalls.

Cash-flow budgets

Cash-flow budgets are similar to operating budgets in that they only cover a one-year period (two years for some governments at the state and local level). However, operating budgets don't differentiate between revenue collected on the first day of the period covered by the budget or the last day. Al long as revenue is collected within the budget period it is not differentiated for operating budget purposes. The same is true for expense outlays. As hinted to by the name, cash-flow budgets pay very close attention to when revenue is collected and when payments are due. These budgets are a further refinement of the operating budget that help ensure that revenue is on hand as payments become due. The most logical way this is achieved is by identifying periods of surplus within the budget period and carrying them to periods of shortfall.

Capital budgets

Operating budgets and cash-flow budgets deal with the day-to-day expenses of a government entity, but capital budgets account of large cash outlays for the purchase of expensive projects that are long lived (over one year). Examples of these types of projects are new buildings at a state university or convention centers. The long life of these types of projects makes them impractical to account for in an operating budget. These projects are typically funded by the government issuing bonds. These bonds are debt instruments sold to the public with specified repayment terms over a predetermined amount of time. Each government entity should define benchmarks that must be met before an expenditure will qualify as a capital project. It is important to think of capital budgets in the context of the government management cycle. Capital budgets are unique in that they not only result in carrying out the goals and objectives of the programming stage, but the projects completed under capital budgets may give rise to new planning goals and objectives.

All three major budget types, operating, cash-flow, and capital, are created as a response to the goals and objectives identified and resources allocated in the programming stage of the government management cycle. However, capital budgets are unique in that they not only result in carrying out the goals and objectives of the programming stage, but the projects completed under capital budgets may give rise to new planning goals and objectives. For example, assume a state government recognizes that to properly carry out its mission, a toll road should be built. This toll road would emerge as a goal from the planning state and measurable objectives to achieve the goal would emerge from the programming state. A capital budget would be developed at the budget state and the toll road would eventually be finished. However, now the toll road needs workers for the tollbooths and people and equipment for maintenance This will require new goals in the planning stage, objectives in the programming stage, and most likely, new operating and cash-flow budgeting for the new toll road workers and equipment.

In the typical scenario, the executive branch submits its budget to the legislative branch. The legislative branch then evaluates the budget and makes changes. The legislative branch then votes on the budget, which once approved by both houses of Congress, is sent back to the executive branch for the chief executive's signature. Once signed by the chief executive (or his veto is overridden by the legislative branch) the appropriated budget becomes law or ordinance. This process applies to all budgets, including capital budgets. In fact, some governments combine operating budgets and capital budgets for the legislative process However, this commingling of budgets can create problems as the legislative process plays out. Because of this, many government entities separate their capital and operating budgets into separate bills or ordinances. In fact, some jurisdictions require this separation by law.

Program based budgets

Generally speaking, since budgets deal directly with the government's expenditure of public funds, safeguards are put into place to limit those expenditures. If the program control is used, then budgets are created and monies allocated to specific projects or "programs." Examples of these programs may include alcohol abuse programs, domestic abuse programs, and English as a second language programs.

Limiting a budget by object class can be thought of as a further refinement of the program limitation. Stated another way, object class limitations will often provide additional budget constraints on funds budgeted for specific programs. For example, the program limitation of a specific amount for an English as a second language program may be further limited as to how much of the total program funds can be expended on salaries for teachers, facilities, and materials.

Fixed or flexible

Budgets can be either fixed or flexible. Where a government entity operates under a fixed budget, operations continue only as long as funds remain in the budget for those operations. Therefore, in the case of a government entity operating under a fixed budget, it is critically important to manage costs or else the overall mission and purpose of the government entity may be in jeopardy. In contrast, a flexible budget is one that can be adjusted for changes in the volume of services or in available revenues, or both. However, despite the added flexibility, it is important to note that strict controls and oversight on spending is still important.

Tracking object classes

Two primary forms of budget controls are based on program and object class. Object class controls provide additional budget constraints on funds budgeted for specific programs. Therefore, from a control standpoint, a government entity benefits from the ability to implement greater numbers of object classes in order to provide greater specificity for expenditure management. Technology (specifically computers and computer software) enable government entities to practically track numerous object classes. To do so, each object class is typically assigned a code. Louisiana State University (LSU) uses an extensive list of object class codes. For example, LSU's expenditure codes are broken down into the following categories: personal services, travel, operation services, supplies, professional services, other charges, capital outlays, debt service, transfers, and foundation. Each of those categories contains dozens of object class codes.

Formal budget making process

The formal budget making process begins with the executive branch issuing its proposed budget to the legislative branch in February (recall that the national government creates a new budget every year). While not at all binding, the executive branch's proposed budget is typically accompanied by voluminous research to support the chief executive's budget proposals. Upon receipt of the executive branch's budget proposal, the budget committees of both the House and the Senate begin drafting their version of the budget resolution. Once the resolutions are finalized, they are brought to their respective floors and voted on for adoption. After the resolutions are adopted, the Senate and the House draft conference reports that detail any differences between the Senate and House versions. The Senate and the House then adopt these reports. Note that the budget resolution is not returned to the chief executive for signing and does not become law. However, the resolution provides the framework within which congressional committees create appropriation bills, which directly fund specific components of the budget. These bills, once agreed upon by Congress, are sent to the chief executive for signing or veto (which the legislative branch can override). Note that the President cannot exercise a line item veto on parts of the budget (some Governors have this power).

Separation of powers

The executive branch initiates the budget making process by drafting a proposed budget. However, this proposed budget is then sent to the legislative branch for approval. During its stay in the legislative branch, the proposed budget often undergoes many changes and modifications (if not wholesale objection). After a final draft of the budget has been created, both houses of Congress vote to approve or disapprove of the proposed budget just as with any proposed legislation. Assuming that the budget is passed by Congress, the executive branch can still exercise its influence via the chief executives veto power. However, as with any other piece of legislation, the legislative branch may override the chief executive's veto and enact the budget without the executive branch's approval. Once the chief executive signs (or his/her veto is overridden) the budget becomes law. The judicial branch settles any disputes that may arise between the executive branch and the legislative branch during the budget process. Also, the reason for government spending and manner of the spending are subject to judicial review to make sure neither the constitution nor laws are violated. Furthermore, the judiciary may decide cases in such a manner that directly affect government spending, creating a financial obligation for the government (e.g., provision of counsel for criminal defendants). Finally, always remember that the citizens themselves possess the ultimate sovereignty in the United States through their voting power.

Direction of the economy

It is true that government in the United States (at all levels) is void of a profit motive. However, seeking a profit is only one reason why predicting the direction of the economy, on a national or local level, would be useful. Perhaps the clearest reason why a government would want to know about shifts in the economy is that such changes can directly affect the government's ability to raise revenue. This anticipated rise or fall of revenue can greatly impact the government's ability to provide services for the community it serves. For example, the national government raises most of its revenue from income tax imposed on the taxable income of its citizens and taxable entities. Therefore, if it is anticipated that the national economy is set to change in a dramatically positive way, it is logical that taxable earnings of its citizens and taxable entities will also increase. This, in turn will lead to greater tax revenues that the national government can consider in the planning, programming, and budgeting stage of the government management cycle.

Economic forecasting is the process of predicting the direction of the economy in whole or in part. As the definition implies, economic forecasting can take place at the world or national level as well as at the local community level. An example of economic forecasting at the local level would be a determination that a large company's factory in a small town would close within the next twelve months. This activity could greatly alter the local economy of this particular community regardless of what is happening at the national or global level. The process of economic forecasting can be achieved by using one or several chosen methods. There are many methods utilized for economic forecasting, but some of the most noted are: extrapolation, identifying indicators, economic base analysis, shift-share analysis, and use of input-output models.

Using social media as a means of communication and providing services

Over the past few years, social media has become an important way for the government to communicate with its citizens. Social media campaigns are quick and easy ways to get information out to the general public. Social media has been used to do the following:

1. Provide information regarding bills being debated in the House or Senate (i.e., create a greater sense of transparency).
2. Obtain information about the needs of constituents (i.e., ensure strategic alignment).
3. Make sure that everyone is aware of the services for which they qualify (i.e., ensure that expensive federal programs are available to everyone who needs them rather than a select few).

Using mobile devices as a means of communication and providing services

Over the past decade, people have become increasing aware that mobile devices contain the necessary global positioning system (GPS) technology to inform those in a given geographic area quickly of an event that impacts them. While there are many who have concerns about the lack of privacy afforded to them when the government accesses this data, there are many cases where using this technology benefits the public, including the following:

1. Sending Amber Alerts (missing children) to cell phones within the area of abduction
2. Alerting the public to impending natural disasters (hurricanes, tornados, tsunamis, etc.)
3. Alerting the public to a dangerous situation (e.g., a bomb threat or a school shooting)
4. Determining where a 911 call is originating from

NIST requirements

The National Institute of Standards and Technology (NIST) is tasked with continuous technological innovation that allows the United States to be competitive and advance scientific measurement, all the while enhancing economic security and improving quality of life. Two of the biggest projects undertaken by this organization include the following:

1. The ability to sync watches and clocks to the exact time of day anywhere in the world
2. Fine-tuning accuracy in global positioning system (GPS) technology

Importance of security and privacy measures

While the advancement in technology has improved our quality of life and ability to communicate with one another, it also puts us at greater risk to have important data stolen and used by those with malicious intent. Most organizations, including the federal government, have implemented data security measures to help prevent hackers from obtaining personal information housed on private servers. However, anytime this information is sent via the Web, there is a risk that it may be purposely intercepted or inadvertently received by others. Therefore, encryption technology is of vital importance. Encryption is the ability to encode messages in a way that only those with the encryption key can view the material.

Interrelationships among planning, programming, budgeting, operations, accounting, reporting and auditing

Government management cycle

The government management cycle began with the traditional management cycle components that are utilized in the private sector. The phases of the traditional model are as follows:

- Planning: This step is where deficiencies are identified and goals are created to eliminate these shortcomings. The goals set at this stage are done so with an eye towards keeping the goals realistic within the context of the organization. Furthermore, steps are identified that will facilitate the accomplishment of the identified goals.
- Organizing: This step follows the planning stage and involves the allocation of capital necessary to achieve the goals developed in the planning stage.
- Directing: This step is where leadership, management, and training are utilized to ensure that both human and financial capital is most efficiently allocated. This stage will involve some delegation of authority while simultaneously retaining accountability for ultimate performance.
- Controlling: The prior steps identify the goals and put mechanisms in place to achieve those goals. This step involves the critique of those mechanisms to ensure that resources are being applied in the most appropriate manner to achieve the identified goals.

Government management cycle vs. the traditional model
The traditional management model has been the standard for organizational management for private sector organizations for a very long time. However, this model required some adjustment for proper application in the public sector context. It is important to note that private sector organizations are driven towards achieving maximum profitability, operate with private funds, and possess the ability to change course very quickly. On the other hand, public sector organizations are driven towards the goal of fulfilling some community need, operate with public funds, and require much more time and energy to change course. As a result of these differences, the government management cycle includes additional steps that provide the public greater accessibility into what the government entity is doing and how it does it. Additionally, the government management cycle includes steps to increase the level of accountability. The government management cycles includes steps to increase the level of accountability. The government management cycle consists of the following steps: planning, programming, budgeting, operations, accounting, reporting, and auditing.

Operations

In the government management cycle, the planning stage yields the broad goals of the government. Next the programming stage sets up specific objectives for achieving those goals. Also in the programming stage, the process of allocating resources in a cost effective way is initiated. Next, a formal budget is made. This budget is law that demonstrates the priorities of community needs performed by the government. After the budget is established, the actual work of achieving the goals and objectives of the government begins. This is the operations stage. It could be said that the operations stage is the apex of the government management cycle in that all of the stages preceding it are in preparation for operations and all of the subsequent stages analyze the results of the operations.

Role of government finance managers
Government finance managers play an important role in the operations stage of the government management cycle. This may seem counterintuitive at first blush. While it is apparent that a government finance manager will play a very important role in the planning, programming, budgeting, accounting, and auditing stages, it would seem that the operations stage would be the primary domain of those government entity components that actually provide the services. It is true that government finance managers may play a secondary role in the operations context; however, their role is still vital in that they oversee operations from a financial standpoint and make sure that no financial controls are violated. Additionally, government finance managers are needed to evaluate the production of the operations stage based on performance criteria.

Internal controls
Internal controls are of extreme importance during the operations phase of the government management cycle. In fact, it can be argued that internal controls are more vital in this stage than in any other stage of the government management cycle. This is due to the fact that any breakdowns in controls at other stages have a chance to be corrected before or after the operations of the government entity are exercised. Control lapses at the operations stage typically mean that some services are performed improperly, not at all, or in such a way that will cause other services to fail (e.g., operating a service at too high of a cost such that the budget is exhausted before other services can be performed). The Government Accountability Office defines internal control "as a process, affected by an agency's management and other personnel, designed to provide reasonable assurance that the objectives of the agency are being achieved in the following categories:

- Effectiveness and efficiency of operations including the use of entities' resources.
- Reliability of financial reporting, including reports on budget execution, financial statements, and other reports for internal and external use.
- Compliance with applicable laws and regulations.

It is certainly true that one of the roles of internal controls is to ensure against loss, fraud, and mismanagement at the operations stage of the government management cycle. However, this is not the only time internal controls are employed. Nothing could be further from the truth. In fact, internal controls should not be viewed as an event, but rather a series of processes that guide a government entity at every stage of the government management cycle. The statement on the front of this card is correct as to operational controls.

<u>Working scenario</u>
The following is but one hypothetical. Keep in mind that the possibilities are nearly endless. Assume that a particular government entity has planned, programmed, and budgeted to build a toll road in their jurisdiction. Now, the operations stage has arrived and it is time to actually begin building. Beginning with management, controls are needed to protect against loss, fraud, and poor management. For example, there could be a level of managerial review for all large decisions (based on time or dollar amount). This would help reduce managerial errors. Next, financial managers would develop internal controls to make sure that each aspect of the project is completed within its budgeted amount. For example, a finance manager would typically break down a project like the construction of a toll road into many different programs and objects codes. Each program and object code would then be monitored to make sure no one item receives too much or too little funding. Finally, operational controls are utilized to oversee the actual production of the project. For example, an internal control requiring the signatures of two managers for purchases of materials and equipment for the toll road's construction could help reduce fraud.

Planning

The first step in the government management cycle is planning. It can be argued that this is the most critical step because all subsequent steps flow, to some extent, from this starting point. At the planning stage, the government entity identifies the goals of the entity and typically prioritizes those goals. Keep in mind that goals identified by government entities generally come from community needs under that government entity's jurisdiction. Prioritizing goals is an especially important component of the planning stage because the needs of the community are often great while the resources available to address those needs are limited. In addition to identifying goals, the planning stage includes determining how those goals will be best achieved.

Stages

The planning stage of the government management cycle has recently become more formal. This trend began in the 1990s specifically with the passage of the Government Performance and Results Act (GPRA). The GPRA affects all stages of the government management cycle, but section three of the GPRA specifically addresses the planning stage. Section three of the GPRA calls for all executive branch agencies to submit strategic plans. These strategic plans are to contain:

- a comprehensive mission statement outlining the major operations of the agency;
- goals and objectives;
- methods for achieving the identified goals and objectives;
- connecting other legally mandated performance goals with the general goals and objectives of the strategic plan;
- identifying specific hurdles to achieving the goals and objectives of the agency that are outside of the agency's control; and
- a description of program evaluations used to establish or revise the agency's goals and objectives, with a schedule for future evaluations.

Note that the GPRA only applies at the national level of government, but state and local governments are also formalizing their planning processes.

Strategic plans

Strategic plans are usually formed during the planning (first) stage of the government management cycle. Strategic plans are an outgrowth of the increased formalization of government management in general and the planning stage of the government management cycle specifically. The national government laid out the requirement that all executive branch agencies create a strategic plan in the Government Performance and Results Act. This act further specified what these strategic plans must include. At the state and local level, strategic plans are also utilized to fine tune the planning stage of the government management cycle. For example, Ivins City, Utah has developed its own strategic planning cycle. This cycle consists of the following steps: community values, community vision, city mission statement, general plan elements, city council legislation, organization development, five year capital improvements plan, annual budget, and evaluation.

Results

The planning stage of the government management cycle is conducted differently among government entities at the same level of government and among different levels of government. With this in mind, planning by most government entities at all levels of government results in the production of a _mission_, a _goal_, and an _objective_. The mission of the government entity is a declaration of the community interests that the entity intends to address. The goals of the government entity disclose desired accomplishments as to specific community interest within the entity's jurisdiction as specified in the entity's mission. Finally, the objectives of a government entity contain specific details as to how the entity intends to meet its

- 29 -

goals. Objectives provide measuring criteria upon which the entity can be evaluated.

An example of this at the state level of government is the Texas Attorney General. This entity lists its mission as acting as the lawyer for the State of Texas. One of the Attorney General's goals is assisting prosecutors with criminal trials. The Attorney General further states the objective that all legal staff will comply with statutory deadlines for timeliness.

Programming

The second stage of the government management cycle (following planning) is programming. Programming is similar to planning in that the achievement of the government entity's goals is the central component of the stage. However, the planning stage focuses on identifying missions, goals, and objectives while the programming stage seeks the most efficient way to achieve the identified goals and objectives. Because objectives provide measurable criteria as to how a government entity will strive to meet its goals, there is considerable overlap between the planning and programming stages with respect to the formulation of objectives. During the programming phase the two guiding principles are: (1) always consider the mission, goals, and objectives (developed in the planning stage) and (2) don't violate the established policies of the chief executive or the legislative branch.

During the planning stage the mission and goals of the government entity are clearly identified. Additionally, the initial development of objectives (strategies, with measurable criteria, for achieving goals) takes place in the planning stage. The programming stage further refines and develops additional objectives. At the beginning of the programming stage a complete list of objectives is established. Following the completion of this list of objectives, strategies are formed to allocate the necessary resources for the successful completion of the government entity's objectives.

Consider the following hypothetical: State A has a Department of Agriculture. The department identifies its mission as "Providing support to the farmers and ranchers of State A." One of the department's goals is to "Provide veterinarian assistance in cases of disease outbreaks in large herds of cattle." An example of an objective for State A's Department of Agriculture could be "To respond to any alerts of disease outbreak in herds of 100 or more cattle within two business days." The department's next step would be to allocate the necessary resources. For example, the department could "Allocate fifteen staff veterinarians to respond to disease outbreaks in herds of one hundred or more cattle.

The programming stage of the government management cycle is very specific to each government entity. This is true because each government entity will have its own distinct mission from which flow specific goals and objectives. However, keep in mind that many of the resources utilized by various government entities overlap.

For example, a state may have a Department of Agriculture and a Department of Transportation. Most likely these departments will have very little in common as far as mission, goals, and objectives are concerned. However, they can both have goals and objectives that require the purchase of similar automobiles. If you assume that the Department of Transportation (in this hypothetical) is vastly more experienced in purchasing automobiles then the Department of Agriculture, it is easy to understand why separate government entities seek input and advice from other government entities in the programming stage of the government management cycle. Always keep in mind that the goal of the programming stage is to achieve goals and objectives in the most efficient manner possible.

<u>Employing private sector entities</u>
Because of the emphasis on achieving goals and objectives efficiently, government entities employ private sector entities to assist in achieving goals and objectives at the programming stage of the government management cycle. Always keep in mind that the goal of the programming stage of the government management cycle is to achieve the goals and objectives of the entity in the most efficient manner possible. Government entities are allowed and, in fact, encouraged to find new ways to achieve their goals and objectives in the most efficient manner possible. One such way that is becoming more prevalent is outsourcing services to private sector entities. A current example of the implementation of this strategy is being undertaken by the United States Treasury Department. Part of this department's goals and objectives include the collection of delinquent tax revenue. In hopes of efficiently reducing the amount of outstanding taxes due, the United States Treasury Department awarded contracts to private sector debt collectors.

Budgeting

The third stage of the government management cycle is budgeting. All levels of government operate with funds collected from its citizens through somewhat limited means (e.g., taxes, fees, and tolls). This differs from the private sector where funds are generated from for-profit activities that are limited only by the imagination of those operating the private sector entities. As a result of this, governments must establish budgets primarily to allocate the monies collected inn the most efficient and beneficial manner as to best address the needs of the community they govern. Because of the competing interests that arise in the budgeting process, budgets are often good indicators as to how a particular government prioritizes community needs and the organization and operations of the government that serve those needs.

The budgeting stage further refines that which is accomplished in the programming stage. For instance, budgets typically only cover one year (sometimes two years at the state level). Additionally, the objectives produced in the programming stage encompass many different components within the government entity while budgets are more narrowly tailored to a specific component within the government entity (e.g., the Internal Revenue has its own distinct budget with the Treasury

Department, which has its own budget with the executive branch). Finally, the budgets that are produced from the budgeting stage are laws and ordinances. The goals and objectives of the programming stage are far less formal.

Just as the budget process is composed of many smaller parts, the government management cycle is also composed of smaller parts, of which budgeting is one. The government management cycle is circular, meaning that the cycle ends where the next cycle begins. The government management cycle begins with the planning and programming stages. In these stages, goals are identified, methods to achieving those goals are structured, and criteria for evaluating the success or failure of the methods employed are determined. It is after the planning and programming stages that a budget is created to assign funds to the various programs created to achieve the identified goals. After the budget is in place, the operations stage begins. As the name indicates, the operations stage is where the actual affirmative steps toward goal achievement take place. During and following the operations stage, the accounting stage begins so as to memorialize how public funds are being utilized to achieve the determined goals as dictated by the budget. The next stage is reporting. Reporting is made in order to inform the public of how their funds were utilized and what was achieved through their expenditure. The reports generated are subject to internal and external auditing. This auditing is the final stage or phase of the government management cycle. However, the results gathers at the conclusion of the auditing stage provide the starting point for the planning stage of the next cycle.

Accounting

The fifth stage of the government management cycle is accounting. Accounting is a term that, broadly speaking, refers to the process of measuring, disclosing or providing assurance about financial information. This financial information helps government managers (and private sector decision makers as well), make decisions at to the allocation of limited resources. The main way that accounting achieves this purpose is through using the double-entry method. This method requires that all transactions are recorded as corresponding credits and debits. These credits and debits must offset each other. This required balance is the assurance that accounting provides. Keep in mind that there are different categories of accounting. These methods include: financial accounting, budgetary accounting, and managerial accounting.

Financial accounting
Within the government context, financial accounting is the branch of accounting that focuses on the preparation of financial statements. Financial statements are a record of the financial flows and levels of the government entity. The major financial statements are the balance sheet, income statement, cash flow statement, and statement of retained earnings. Not all of these types of financial statements are relevant for government entities. Financial accounting and the reports it produces, assist government managers in properly assessing the financial well-being of their government entity. The information used to compile financial reports under this

method of accounting is typically obtained from transactions entered into during the operations stage of the government management cycle. Financial accounting is subject to uniform standards that are established and overseen by independent organizations. At the national level, this oversight body is the Federal Accounting Standards Advisory Board. At the state and local level, the Governmental Accounting Standards Board determines the standards.

Budgetary accounting
It is important to remember that the appropriated budget is law. With this in mind, the role of budgetary accounting is not only to track the flows of funds, but to keep the government entity in compliance with the law. In order to do so, budgetary accounting tracks the budget itself. Because the budget typically describes the purpose for which money is to be spent, the amount to be spent on such purpose, and the time of such expenditure, budgetary accounting will track the various money flows of the entity in the same manner. Budgetary accounting helps those involved in the planning, programming, and operations stages of the government management cycle understand their capabilities and restraints with regard to the expenditure of resources to achieve the entity's goals and objectives.

Managerial accounting
The Chartered Institute of Management Accountants defines management accounting as "The process of identification, measurement, accumulation, analysis, preparation, interpretation and communication of information used by management to plan, evaluate and control within an entity and to assure appropriate use of and accountability for its resources. Management accounting also comprises the preparation of financial reports for non management groups such as shareholders, creditors, regulatory agencies and tax authorities." Managerial accounting differs from financial and budgetary accounting in that managerial accounting is not subject to strict external standards. As such, the management of a particular government entity can devise its own system of measures that will best assist them in determining the efficiency of their entity's operations. Because of this flexibility, managerial accounting systems can be tailor made to best reflect the operations of each particular government entity. In devising a managerial accounting system, managerial accountants will often utilize both financial and non-financial data.

Reporting

The sixth stage of the government management cycle is reporting. This stage is critical in order for a government entity to communicate its operations. Specifically, government reports consist of various types of proclamations as to the efficiency with which the government entity utilized its budgeted resources to accomplish its goals and objectives. The form and focus of these various reports will differ depending on whether they are internal or external. Generally, external reports communicate the effectiveness of the government entity to the public while internal reports assist the government entity's management make decisions.

External financial reporting

The purpose of external financial reports issued by government entities is to communicate the effectiveness of that entity to the public. Stated differently, external financial reporting reveals a government entity's level of success in achieving its goals and objectives through efficient allocation of limited public resources. External reports serve to not only communicate this information to the public, but also to provide accountability. Because of the importance of these external reports, standards are in place to make sure that they are properly prepared so as to serve their purpose. External financial reports are subject to the Generally Accepted Accounting Principles (GAAP). Different organizations define the GAAP for different types of entities.

The foundational requirement is that external financial reports comport with the Generally Accepted Accounting Principles (GAAP). Different organizations define the GAAP for entities at different levels of government. These organizations are: Governmental Accounting Standards Board (GASB): The GASB was "organized in 1984 as an operating entity of the Financial Accounting Foundation (FAF) to establish standards of financial accounting and reporting for state and local governmental entities." Therefore, the GASB establishes the GAAP for state and local entities.

"The mission of the FASAB is to promulgate [national] accounting standards after considering the financial and budgetary information needs of citizens, congressional oversight groups, executive agencies, and the needs of other users of [national] financial information." Therefore, the FASAB establishes the GAAP for the national government and its entities. (Information taken from http://www.fasab.gov.)

FASB establishes the GAAP for the private sector and states the following as its mission: "The mission of the Financial Accounting Standards Board is to establish and improve standards of financial accounting and reporting for the guidance and education of the public, including issuers, auditors, and users of financial information. (Information taken from http://www.fasb.org.)

Types of external financial reports
- GAAP Reports. These reports are basically generic external financial reports. These reports are fairly technical in nature and are intended primarily for government overseers (e.g., member of Congress, watchdog groups, etc.). In addition to GAAP, additional reporting standards may be imposed on these reports.
- Special purpose financial reports. These reports are typically not intended to be complete financial reports pursuant to GAAP (as is the case with GAAP reports). Instead, these reports are intended for a limited audience and cover limited transactions. For example, the State of Florida issued a special purpose financial report to comply with the provisions of a grant agreement

FREE Study Skills DVD Offer

Dear Customer,

Thank you for your purchase from Mometrix! We consider it an honor and privilege that you have purchased our product and want to ensure your satisfaction.

As a way of showing our appreciation and to help us better serve you, we have developed a Study Skills DVD that we would like to give you for <u>FREE</u>. **This DVD covers our "best practices" for studying for your exam, from using our study materials to preparing for the day of the test.**

All that we ask is that you email us your feedback that would describe your experience so far with our product. Good, bad or indifferent, we want to know what you think!

To get your **FREE Study Skills DVD**, email <u>freedvd@mometrix.com</u> with "FREE STUDY SKILLS DVD" in the subject line and the following information in the body of the email:

    a. The name of the product you purchased.

    b. Your product rating on a scale of 1-5, with 5 being the highest rating.

    c. Your feedback. It can be long, short, or anything in-between, just your impressions and experience so far with our product. Good feedback might include how our study material met your needs and will highlight features of the product that you found helpful.

    d. Your full name and shipping address where you would like us to send your free DVD.

If you have any questions or concerns, please don't hesitate to contact me directly.

Thanks again!

Sincerely,

Jay Willis
Vice President
<u>jay.willis@mometrix.com</u>
1-800-673-8175

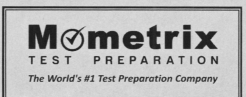

between the Florida Department of Environmental Protection and the United States Environmental Protection Agency.

- Popular reports. These reports are more focused on the role of public disclosure in that they are typically drafted such that a layman not well versed in accounting terminology can readily understand them. The Government Finance Officers Association (GFOA) provides a detailed list of recommendations on the drafting of such reports at: http://www.gfoa.org/services/rp/documents/preparingpopreports.pdf

Non-financial external reports

Included in non-financial external reports are popular reports and performance reports. Popular reports are often a mix of both financial and non-financial reporting. Their main objective is to communicate with less accounting savvy citizens. In doing so, popular reports may include both financial and non-financial information. Performance reports are designed to pick up where GAAP reports leave off. GAAP reports, in extreme detail, demonstrate how public funds were expended during the relevant reporting period. However, GAAP reports do not illustrate the results of these expenditures. Therefore, performance reports connect the outflow of resources to their results. At the national level, performance reporting is required. This results in certain uniformity in national level performance reports. However, state and local governments are not required to apply GAAP to their performance reports. Therefore, performance reports at the state and local level differ greatly among jurisdictions.

Accountability

Government entities produce external reports for many different reasons. These include the desire (or requirement) to inform the public and the necessity to report on achievements so that the entity may be held accountable. However, while the government entity may benefit from the production of these external reports, as well as the reports themselves, the external reports are not specifically geared for the benefit of the entity. Instead, this role belongs to internal reports. Rather than adhering to a strict format, managers of government entities may produce internal reports that arrange or compile data in any way that is useful to them.

External vs. internal government reports

- Role. The role of external reports is vastly different between external and internal reporting. In the case of external reports, their main role is to inform the public as to the entity's operations. This reporting helps insure that the entity is accountable for its utilization of public funds. However, internal reports are strictly for the use and benefit of the decision makers within the government entity itself.
- Rate of Occurrence. Because of the standardized nature of external reports, it should not be surprising that most external reports have a dictated rate of occurrence. These reports are typically required at the end of a specified period (after completion of the operations stage of the government

management cycle). On the other hand, internal reports can be produced whenever the government entity's management decides they would be of the most use.

- Form. The form of external reports is outlined by GAAP. All external reports must conform to GAAP requirements. Additionally, some external reports may have additional statutory reporting requirements that must be followed if the law requiring the report so specifies. Again, internal reports are extremely flexible and may take whatever form best serves the government entity's management.

Impact

As is the case with all of the stages of the government management cycle, the reporting stage greatly impacts all of the other stages of the cycle. For instance, the greatest concern during the operations stage is that community needs are being properly addressed in the most efficient manner possible with respect to resources. If the reports generated in the reporting stage of the government management cycle are produced quickly enough, any inefficiencies may be determined and corrected while operations are still taking place. Additionally, the reports generated during the reporting stage form the starting place for the auditors to do their job in the auditing stage of the government management cycle.

Recent trends

Within recent years there has been a trend towards performance reports. Performance reports may include financial data, but are very different from financial reports that are also produced in the reporting stage. For example, both performance and financial reports are created to measure the effectiveness of a particular government entity; however it is very difficult to achieve this goal through pure financial analysis. Additional information is needed to truly measure whether or not the government entity has achieved its goals and objectives. This additional information appears in performance reports in the form of results of operations of the government entity. The financial reports will show cash flows to the penny, but often fail to demonstrate the final results of those cash flows (e.g., the building was fifty percent completed, the toll road was finished on time, etc.). The Association of Government Accountants provides two programs to encourage the use of performance reports: the CEAR program (national level) and the SEA program (state and local level).

Producing performance reports

By comparison, financial reports are simpler (not necessarily easier to produce) than performance reports. Because financial reports deal strictly with financial data and are vehicles for ensuring accountability of the government entity producing them, typically management, finance managers, and accountants are parties involved with the production of financial reports. However, because performance reports deal with financial data in addition to voluminous data that demonstrate the results of the entity's operations many more parties are involved in the production of performance reports. For instance, those that are in charge of the operations of the entity will have to input their data into the reports Additionally, the critical members of the planning and programming stages of the government management cycle will have to input data so that the performance report clearly reflects the success (or lack thereof) with which the entity addressed its goals and objectives. Additionally, human resources specialists are needed to evaluate the effectiveness with which the government entity's people were utilized. Furthermore, auditors as well as all of the financial parties involved with the production of the financial reports will be called upon to contribute. Outside of the entity, even law makers, members of the public, and those doing business with the entity may have information that is valuable to the production of a quality performance report.

Guidelines
Currently, there are no formal standards for performance reporting at the state and local level. However, the Governmental Accounting Services Board (GASB) has developed some guiding principles for the creation of performance reports. For example, according to the GASB the foundation of a performance report consists of two things: (1) service efforts, and (2) accomplishments. Service efforts deal with the allocation of resources to perform operations necessary to achieve the goals and objectives of the government entity. For example, service efforts would track the number of man hours spent on a particular activity. The accomplishments component focuses on the results of the operations undertaken by the government entity. These results are further subdivided into any actual tangible product or service rendered by the entity (sometimes referred to as outputs) as well as the community needs that were (or were not) addressed by the operations of the entity (sometimes referred to as outcomes). It should be noted that the national government emphasizes these same points in its performance reporting.

Service efforts
Service efforts and accomplishments are linked to indicate the true performance of a government entity. Without this link, a distorted picture emerges. On one hand, if just service efforts are examined, only the expenditures to achieve a goal or objective are viewed with no idea of how effective these expenditures were in achieving the goal or objective. Similarly, if accomplishments are taken alone, then there is no indication as to how efficiently resources were utilized to achieve the accomplishments. This is where the concepts of cost-effectiveness and cost-efficiency come into play. Cost-effectiveness measures the amount of resources allocated to each community need addressed by the entity (outcome). Cost-efficiency measures the resources allocated to each tangible product or service produced by the entity (output).

The potential for examples here is almost limitless. For continuity, let's revisit our toll road example. The toll road project is a result of a government entity's (probably manner entities) planning, programming, and operations. Assume that the toll road was constructed by the State A Highway Department. Furthermore, let's assume that the project was begun and finished in the same reporting period. During and immediately following the operations stage, preparation of performance reports has begun. Since these reports are composed by a state level entity (State A Highway Department), there are no formal standards that these reports must follow, but State A chooses to follow the GASB guidelines. Therefore, some of the service efforts tracked in the performance report(s) will include how many man hours were spent on the project, the allocation of machinery and other entity hard assets to the project, and the amount of budgeted funds directed to the construction of the toll road. Meanwhile, the accomplishments documented in the performance report may include a detailed description of the toll road itself (e.g., ten miles long with three lanes in each direction) and the community needs addressed by the toll road (e.g., traffic congestion in the area is reduced by twenty percent).

Formal standards
Unlike the state and local levels of government, the national level of government is governed by formal standards with regard to performance reporting. Primarily there are two sources for these national level standards: (A) the Government Performance and Results Act of 1993 (GPRA), and (B) the Federal Accounting Standards Advisory Board's *Statement of Federal Financial Accounting Standards 15: Management's Discussion and Analysis* (Statement).

- GPRA: The stated purpose of the GPRA is "To provide for the establishment of strategic planning and performance measurement in the Federal Government, and for other purposes."[1]

(Information taken from http://www.whitehouse.gov/omb/mgmt-gpra/gplaw2m.html)

- Statement: The Statement "establishes standards for preparing Management's Discussion and Analysis (MD&A). MD&A is an important vehicle for (1) communicating managers' insights about the reporting entity, (2) increasing the understandability and usefulness of the general purpose federal financial report (GPFFR), and (3) providing understandable and accessible information about the entity and its operations, service levels, successes, challenges, and future. Some federal agencies also refer to MD&A as the "overview." (Information taken from http://www.fasab.gov/pdffiles/15_md&a.pdf)

Standards at the national level
The GPRA specifically requires that each agency complete its performance report by March 31 of each year. Additionally, these reports must include performance indicators which link the identified performance goals with performance achievements for the year at issue. For comparison, the GPRA also requires that the results from all preceding years (beginning with the year of the GPRA's enactment) be included in the current year's report. Finally, the GPRA requires detailed identification of targets that were not met and why they were not met. Other contents of the performance report may include information showing whether efficiency and effectiveness are improving or worsening between reporting periods,

and detailing the performance of other government entities for comparison (where appropriate).

<u>Comparative data</u>
An effective tool in performance reporting can be the comparison of results among separate government entities. However, there are many variables that must be accounted for before such a comparison is valid. An example may best demonstrate this. Assume that State A's Highway Department is compiling its performance report for the construction of a toll road. Because there are many toll road projects taking place at any given time around the country, it is tempting for State A to use other entities' data for comparison purposes (especially where State A looks good by comparison). Before including any of this other data, State A should analyze the distinguishing factors that exist in other jurisdictions. For example, State A may want to utilize data from State B's toll road project to illustrate how much less money State A spent on labor. However, further analysis may reveal that the cost of living in State B is much higher than in State A, therefore, comparison of labor costs is ineffective. Additionally, State A could artificially look good by comparison due to the fact that they entered the project with much more equipment (perhaps acquired to complete prior projects) than a comparative jurisdiction. There could also be distinguishing factors among the projects themselves (e.g., the nature of the land that the toll road is built on).

<u>Communicative goals</u>
Financial reporting is almost exclusively quantitative in nature. That is, numbers are used to identify dollars allocated to a project and dollars spent on a project. Stated differently, success at the financial reporting level is achieved if the money spent on a program is at or less than the amount budgeted for that program. The goal of performance reporting is much different. Performance reporting does include quantitative data, but only as a sub-component of a qualitative analysis. Put another way, the performance report doesn't stop at the question "how much did we spend," but continues to ask "what did we get for our money." As a result of this different focus, narratives are an important part of performance reports. It is often these narratives that provide the context for the quantitative data. Proper utilization of narratives allows the performance report to link service efforts and outcomes.

Auditing

An audit may be defined as a formal investigation or systematic check or assessment at to efficiency, effectiveness, or compliance. It is important to remember that while there are many connotations that come to mind when the word "audit" is used, it is a very broad term that can be used in many different contexts. As such, there are several different types of audits that seek to achieve distinct results. For example, there are external audits (which consist of financial audits, attestation engagements, and performance audits) and internal audits. These different types of audits are distinguishable by their goals and levels of formality.

External audits

External audits consist of financial audits, attestation engagements, and performance audits. As would be expected, the auditing stage of the government management cycle is subject to fairly strict standards. In the case of external audits there are two primary entities that put forth standards: (1) the American Institute of Certified Public Accountants (AICPA), and (2) the Government Accountability Office (GAO). The AICPA sets out its standards in the form of Generally Accepted Auditing Standards (GAAS). GAAS is made up of ten items covering general standards, standards of field work, and standards of reporting, along with interpretations. GAAS is created for non-government entities but is influential in determining standards for government audits. The GAO created standards called the Generally Accepted Government Auditing Standards (GAGAS). The standards adopted by GAGAS apply to financial audits, attestation engagements, and performance audits at the national, state, and local level of government.

Example of external audits

Let's revisit our toll road example. From an external audit perspective, perhaps the most visible audit would be the financial audit. Both types of financial audits would no doubt take place. First, a financial statement audit would be conducted. This audit would apply GAAP to determine the reliability of data and processes used by the highway department to produce their financial statements on the toll road project. Additionally, there would be financial related audits. These audits would make sure that financial information was reported within pre-established criteria, specific financial compliance requirements are adhered to, and/or the suitability of the government entity's internal controls. Next, there would certainly be attestation engagements. On a project like the construction of a toll road, there are many contracts awarded. This is fertile ground for an attestation engagement to determine whether internal controls are appropriate to prohibit overpaying for services. Finally, performance audits would occur to track the entity's economy and efficiency and that the goals of the program are being achieved. Remember that the hallmark of external auditing is strict standards and uniformity.

Attestation engagements

Attestation engagements can be part of financial or non-financial (e.g., performance) audits. Attestation engagements involve the review or application of pre-determined procedures on a subject matter, or an assertion about the subject matter. Attestation engagements can cover a broad range of topics, some of which include: an entity's internal financial reporting, an entity's compliance with laws and regulations, an entity's internal control over compliance, the reliability of an entity's performance measures, the appropriateness of an entity's contract amounts, etc. Attestation engagements are expected to comply with standards established by the AICPA.

Performance audits

Performance audits are external audits that seek to evaluate a specific organization, program, or function based on objective data. As with all external audits, a primary objective of performance audits is to provide accountability and to assist government entity decision makers. There are two types of performance audits: (1) economy and efficiency audits, and (2) program audits. Economy and efficiency audits detail how well an entity is acquiring and utilizing its resources, the reasons behind any inefficiencies, and whether laws and regulations have been complied with. Program audits address the extent to which the program's purpose is being achieved, the effectiveness of organizations, programs, activities, and functions, and whether or not the entity has complied with the laws that apply to the program.

Government accountability

The government entity (national level) that is charged with the duty of overseeing government accountability is the Government Accountability Office (GAO). Interestingly, while the major government agencies are in the executive branch, the GAO is in the legislative branch. The GAO is a non-partisan agency that evaluates the executive branch agencies to oversee their expenditure of public funds and to evaluate how well they achieve their goals. The specific purpose of the GAO is to accumulate and present data to legislators so that members of Congress will be best equipped to make policy decisions regarding executive branch agencies. The GOA is very prolific and issued more than one thousand reports each year.

Internal audits

As opposed to external audits which are conducted by independent auditors to measure the efficiency and effectiveness of an agency's management, internal audits largely conducted by managers of the agency. As such, internal auditors are typically far less independent from management than external auditors (although some independence must exist for the internal audit to be useful). An important difference between internal and external audits is that internal audits are not conducted specifically for the public's benefit (although people outside of the entity can obtain internal audit results through legal means). However, despite this difference, internal audits are often conducted in much the same fashion as external audits. This methodology permits the entity's management have reasonably accurate idea of the results of external audits. Additionally, the entity's management can identify and remedy any problems with internal controls.

Audits

Government financial audits are actually a broad category that includes several types of audits. Specifically, government financial audits include: (1) financial statement audits and (2) financial related audits. Financial statement audits are conducted primarily to make sure that the various financial statements produced by a government entity are produced in such a way as to provide an accurate measure of the entity's financial position, results of operations, and cash flows. To assure of this accuracy, Generally Accepted Accounting Principles (GAAP) are applied. Financial related audits are different in that they typically involve whether or not financial information is presented in accordance within a pre-established criteria, specific financial compliance requirements are adhered to, and/or the suitability of the government entity's internal controls. Keep in mind that government financial audits are external audits.

Governmental financing process

Government finance

Simply put, government finance is the utilization of public funds by the government to achieve the various goals and objectives identified by its various entities. This activity is of critical importance because the funds available to government entities are very limited while the public needs are nearly unlimited. Unlike the private sector, where entities can creatively find new ways to generate revenue, government entities are limited in how they acquire funds to carry out their purposes. Specifically, government entities acquire resources by taxing citizens and private entities, charging user fees, obtaining grants or sharing revenues from other levels of government, and by issuing debt instruments. As expected, each resource stream is fraught with limitations (both legal and practical) and complexities.

Tax policy concern of tax equity

Much time is spent determining the various economic affects of taxation. However, before any tax can be administered, there must be tax equity. This concept refers to the fairness of the tax as applied to the taxed group. In other words, the concept of tax equity doesn't focus on the tax itself, but rather that the imposition of the tax is done fairly. This concept is most easily seen in the area of income taxes. In order to achieve tax equity on income taxes, the United States government imposes different rates of tax on different levels of income. This concept is also referred to as graduated taxation. As the individual's income increases, that income is subject to increasing rates of tax. This form of tax equity is often expressed in terms of vertical tax equity (increasing taxes on those with a greater ability to pay) or horizontal tax equity (taxing those with a similar capacity to pay the same amount). The concept of tax equity also applies to business entities.

Tax policy of tax equity does not apply
While the United States applies graduated rates in the context of the income tax imposed at the national level, many taxes do not apply such tax equity measures. For example, property taxes (imposed at the state and local level) are "flat." This means that no matter who owns the property (rich or poor) the same amount of tax is applied to that property. Often, this lack of tax equity is more theoretical than actual because property taxes are based on assessed values of the property subject to the tax. Because people with higher incomes or wealth levels tend to own higher valued property, tax equity actually exists. However, this is not always the case. Many state and local governments impose sales taxes. These sales taxes are typically applied to the purchase of mundane items such as toothpaste and tissue paper. Both rich and poor purchase these items and the sales tax is imposed on everyone regardless of there net worth. Therefore, these taxes (flat taxes in

general) are deemed regressive as opposed to the progressive graduated income tax regime.

Who is affected

Tax equity is the tax policy concern that evaluates the fairness of taxes based on whether the levy is appropriate given the level of income, wealth, or other measuring factor of the taxed parties. However, just because a tax is levied in an equitable way doesn't foreclose other tax policy considerations. For example, suppose that a government entity seeks to complete a project that benefits a small readily identifiable group of citizens. Is it logical to tax all the citizens of the government entities jurisdiction just for the benefit of this small group? This question represents an ever-present balancing act that government entities constantly juggle. To illustrate this issue, it makes sense to revisit the toll road project undertaken by State A. In the case of most toll roads, the tax policy issue of benefits received is a driving force in electing to operate a toll road. This is because most toll roads are built with little or no general tax funds, but instead charge tolls to pay for the construction of the project. Obviously, those who benefit from the road's construction, its drivers, pay the tolls.

Effective tax policy

Effective tax policy requires more than just implementation of an equitable tax regime imposed on those who benefit most from the provisions of government entities. Governments must also factor in tax collection. For example, an otherwise brilliant tax policy is irrelevant if the taxes imposed are inefficient to collect or difficult to collect for other reasons. To illustrate this point, one can look at real property taxes. Many states impose real property taxes. These taxes are a substantial part of these states' revenue. To simplify their collection of these taxes, many states allow counties and local school districts to impose the taxes. This reduces the inefficiency of a state collecting all of the real property taxes and then filtering the funds down to the counties and states. A further example of collection factoring into tax policy is seen in the collection of income taxes at the national level. The vast majority of these taxes are required to be withheld from paychecks of individual citizens. The individual citizens must independently seek any refund of this amount.

Social and economic goals

The main function of taxes is to collect revenue so that the government can meet the needs of its citizens. To this end, economic goals are a critical component of tax policy. However, the influence of economic goals is not limited to the government's desire to raise the most revenue. In addition, a particular government entity (or level of government) may desire to affect the economy in a way that only indirectly increases tax revenues. For example, recently the national government passed a law that capped the taxes on dividends at fifteen percent (well below the top tax brackets applied to other forms of income). The policy behind this bill passage was the national government's desire to increase capital investment in the private

- 44 -

sector. Of course, an ancillary benefit of this law could be increased tax revenues as a result of the increase in private investment. Additionally, social goals often steer tax policy. An example of this is the national government's provision of a charitable contribution deduction. This law actually reduces government tax revenue, but this negative is outweighed by the governmental interest of encouraging contributions to charities which often perform services that the government would otherwise be responsible for.

Tax expenditures

Tax expenditures are special tax provisions that are designed to accomplish some social or economic goal without regard to tax equality. They are like "entitlements" because they are not subject to annual budget appropriations, but are paid out to any business or individual that meets the eligibility rules, regardless of the total cost to the government. Politically, tax expenditures can be favorable to entitlement programs because they are classified as tax cuts and not entitlement programs. However, their affect is pretty much the same. An example of a tax expenditure at the national level is the earned income credit. This credit provides reduction in taxes owed by low income families. Additionally, the earned income credit is what is known as a refundable credit. This means that if there is left over credit amount after all of the low income families tax obligation has been eliminated, the family may obtain a refund in the amount of the excess credit This provision highlights that the social goal of assisting low income families trumps the government's desire to raise revenue (in this particular case).

Dedicated tax

The term dedicated tax (a.k.a., earmarked tax or restricted tax) refers to a tax that is imposed for a specific purpose carved out from the general revenues collected by a government entity. This differs from ordinary taxes that are collected for the general needs of the government entity. The revenue generated by a dedicated tax is typically placed into a restricted fund that is accessible only for the stated purpose for which the taxes were collected. An example of a dedicated tax is found in the state of Pennsylvania. In this state there is a dedicated alcohol tax collected solely to support the treatment and prevention of alcohol and other drug addictions. Accordingly, all alcohol taxes collected by the state of Pennsylvania go into a specific fund to be accessed only for the stated purpose of the tax. It should be noted that these dedicated funds may be borrowed against for non-dedicated uses. But these borrowed amounts must be repaid to the dedicated fund (often with interest).

Income tax

The income tax is one of the three broad classifications of tax (wealth tax and consumption tax being the others). Income taxes represent the largest source of revenue for the national government. Additionally, many states and some localities also implement an income tax. The income tax at all levels of government achieves tax equality by applying gradually increasing rates of tax to higher levels of income. This makes the income tax a "progressive" tax. Further enhancing its tax equity, the income tax affords those who qualify various deductions, exemptions, and credits. It should be noted that corporations are also subject to income taxes. Furthermore, corporate income taxes are also imposed at graduated rate (although these rates are much "flatter" than individual income tax rates). An example of an income tax that is not progressive is the payroll tax which funds Social Security and Medicare. These taxes are regressive in that they impose the same rate of tax over a broad scope of income levels.

<u>Advantages</u>
There are various advantages that an income tax provides both the government imposing the income tax and the citizens and business entities subject to it. For instance, from the government's point of view, the income tax is effective at taxing the vast majority of its working aged citizens and profitable entities. With more citizens and entities taxed, sufficient government resources can be generated without imposing too heavy a burden on any one group. Also, governments can easily manipulate income taxes to encourage or discourage certain types of behavior. For example, deductions are allowed for income diverted to a qualified retirement account to encourage saving for retirement. Furthermore, because the vast majority of United States citizens earn the majority of their money in the form of salary that is subject to withholding, income taxes are easily collected. From the citizens/entities standpoint, one advantage of the income tax is that it automatically adjusts to their status in the market. In other words, if an individual is unemployed and earns no income, he/she owes no income tax (and may even be allowed assistance in the form of a credit).

Wealth taxes

Wealth taxes are one of the three broad categories of taxes that governments implement to raise revenue (income and consumption are the other two). Wealth taxes differ from income taxes and consumption taxes in that they typically do not implement a tax on a transaction. Instead, a wealth tax attempts to tax the assessed value of something. Examples of wealth taxes are real property taxes, personal property taxes, estate taxes, capital gains taxes, and the taxation of intangibles. The national government currently utilizes only two types of wealth taxes: capital gains taxes and estate taxes. State and local governments rely heavily on wealth taxes, property taxes specifically. Property taxes generally pay for schools and other local and state level services. The benefit for states and localities relying on property taxes is that the subject of the tax is generally immobile. Therefore, unlike income and consumption taxes, the subject of the property tax cannot easily be taken out of the jurisdiction.

<u>Personal property taxes</u>
Like real property taxes, personal property taxes are wealth taxes. However, the property subject to personal property taxes is very different from real property.

- 46 -

While real property is fixed, personal property is highly mobile. Personal property includes even minor household items and personal effects, but most state and local governments that impose personal property taxes exempt these items from personal property taxes. However, if similar items are used in a business, then the personal property tax will apply. In the business context, exceptions are made for inventory and intangible property such as copyrights or patents. Often, governments that impose a personal property tax (the national government does not impose a personal property tax) will utilize the same rates as applied in real property taxes (for example the State of Washington). Governments confront an even worse problem with valuation of personal property than with real property because it is very difficult to determine if full disclosure of personal property has taken place and there are so many types of personal property.

Problems with administering a property tax
Property taxes are probably the most commonly used form of wealth taxes. Additionally, property taxes usually are the greatest generator of government revenue at the state and local level. Unfortunately, property taxes are not without their drawbacks to both the citizens and businesses paying them and the governments imposing them. From the government's point of view, one of the greatest hurdles to properly implementing a property tax is the issue of assessment. In order for a property tax to be effective, the tax must be assessed on an accurate measure of the value of the property. This requires periodic determinations of property values. Not only is this process expensive and time consuming (professional appraisers must be hired), but it is also speculative. From the perspective of property owners, property taxes can prove overly burdensome when property values rise (therefore, increasing property taxes) without a corresponding increase in income or other funds necessary to pay the tax. This can happen in states or localities where a "hot" property market develops. Typically this problem is remedied by citizens voting into effect equalization or other laws aimed at limiting the amount of increase attributed to property values within a given period of time.

Determinations
The following is an example of property tax determinations at the individual level. Debra is a citizen of State A. State A imposes a property tax. Both the land and improvements to the land (e.g., buildings) are subject to the property tax. Debra bought her house earlier this year for $100,000. State A's property tax rate is 1.6% (sometimes stated as 16 mills). Therefore, Debra's current year property tax obligation will be $1,600 (.016 x 100,000). The following year, State A's Tax Assessor determines that Debra's house has appreciated to a value of $150,000. Furthermore, State A's property tax rate holds steady at 1.6%. The following year's property tax obligation for Debra is $2,400 (.016 x 150.000). However, assume that State A has passed a law capping the increase in the valuation of any residential real property at 10% for any given year. Now, despite Debra's determined value of $150,000, the value used for property tax purposes is $110,000 (100,000 x 1.1). This results in Debra's property tax obligation coming to $1,760 (110,000 x .016).

Intangibles tax

An intangibles tax is a wealth tax imposed on the value of intangibles. In this respect it is similar to the taxes imposed on personal and real property. Intangibles are more mobile than real property. In fact, because intangibles exist only in theory or "on paper" they can be located anywhere in the world without any inconvenience to their owner. The national government does not impose an intangibles tax. Therefore, only state and local levels of government apply such taxes. Even within the same level of government, the application of an intangibles tax can vary greatly. For example, Florida imposes an intangibles tax on the value of certain financial assets (including stocks and bonds). Once a value for these intangibles is determined, a tax rate is applied to the value to determine the tax due. However, in Kansas local government applies what they call an intangibles tax to earnings received from intangible assets (e.g., savings accounts, stocks, bonds, accounts receivables, and mortgages). Because this tax is imposed on the earnings and not the actual value of the intangibles, it is questionable whether this tax is a wealth based intangibles tax or misnamed income tax.

Inheritance and estate taxes

Both inheritance and estate taxes are wealth taxes. Inheritance and estate taxes are similar in that they both impose taxation at the point when a decedent's estate passes to his/her heirs and assigns. This feature makes these taxes somewhat unique compared to other wealth taxes which are not transactional in nature. Despite their similar names, inheritance and estate taxes are very different. They are distinguished by who the tax is imposed on. In the case of the inheritance tax, those inheriting the wealth are subject to the tax. In the case of the estate tax, the estate itself is subject to the tax (however it should be noted that property passing to the heirs and assigns is subject to liens if the estate tax is not paid). The national level of government applies only an estate tax (coupled with a gift tax to maintain the integrity of the regime). States may impose both inheritance and estate taxes. Mainly due to political pressures, the role of inheritance and estate taxes has been curtailed at the national and state level in recent years.

Consumption taxes

In broad terms there are three types of taxes: income taxes, wealth taxes, and consumption taxes. Consumption taxes are distinguishable from the other forms of taxation (as typically imposed) in that they are inherently more regressive. That is to say, the tax burden that results from a consumption tax is imposed with little regard to the taxed party's ability to pay. However, despite this apparent inequity, consumption taxes are viewed as fair in that they only tax those who enter into the specific transactions that are subject to the consumption tax. This, at least in theory, gives taxpayers some degree of control over their tax burdens. For example, if a citizen doesn't wish to pay, or is unable to pay a sales tax (a type of consumption tax), that citizen is free to not purchase the goods subject to the sales tax. The argument exists that some things potentially subject to consumption taxes are not really optional (e.g., the purchase of food) thereby accentuating the regressive nature of consumption taxes. However, most jurisdictions make exceptions for certain items deemed to be necessities to lessen this regressiveness. The typical types of consumption taxes are: sales taxes, use taxes, excise taxes, and value added taxes.

Use taxes

A use tax is another form of a consumption tax. In theory, a use tax is very similar to a sales tax. In fact, most academic treatises discuss "sales and use taxes" simultaneously. From an application perspective, use taxes are typically applied in the same fashion as sales taxes. Use taxes are generally levied by multiplying a tax rate by the assessed value of an item. The main difference between a sales and a use tax is often timing. While a sales tax is levied at the moment an item (subject to the sales tax) is purchased, a use tax is charged by a specific jurisdiction once such an item is brought within that jurisdiction. As such, use taxes are often used by a jurisdiction to protect the revenue that would otherwise be generated by sales taxes from erosion by residents buying goods in other jurisdictions. However, to keep sales and use taxes from being too burdensome on citizens, there is often a credit that applies to the use tax equal to the amount of sales tax charged (although some items are often exempted). Use taxes are primarily charged at the state level and, can be difficult to enforce when citizens do not willingly disclose the requisite information needed to impose the tax.

Excise taxes to sales taxes

Like sales taxes, excise taxes are another type of consumption tax. Additionally, excise taxes are charged to consumers at the point of sale or some other predetermined point of time (e.g., at the beginning of the year for annual excise taxes). Excise taxes are most distinguishable from sales taxes in that they are more focused than sales taxes. Generally, sales taxes apply to sales of all goods with some exceptions. However, excise taxes only apply to specific transactions. Additionally, sales tax revenue is typically included in the taxing jurisdiction's general account for discretionary use. Excise taxes are often placed into special accounts that fund specific projects. Excise taxes may be implemented to achieve several different goals of the taxing jurisdiction. For example, the "thing" subject to an excise tax may require greater expenditures by the taxing jurisdiction. This would be the case where an excise tax is imposed on a certain license that requires greater government oversight. The excise tax is intended to offset those costs. Also, excise taxes have been used to dissuade certain behaviors (e.g., smoking, drinking, and gambling).

Sales taxes

Sales taxes can be imposed at the national, state, or local levels. Currently, there is no national level sales tax. States and localities differ widely on how (and if) they chose to apply a sales tax. For instance, some jurisdictions will impose a blanket sales tax on the sale of all goods. Often, these governments will seek to soften the regressive nature of such a tax burden by exempting certain necessities from the sales tax (e.g., clothing under a certain price). Some governments make sales of services subject to their sales tax. A good example of how a sales tax is applied is the State of Texas (which does not impose a state or local level income tax). At the state level, Texas imposes a sales tax on all retail sales, leases and rentals of most goods, as well as taxable services. Texas counties have the option of imposing an additional local sales tax for a combined total of state and local taxes of 8 1/4%. Texas cities also have the option of imposing an additional local sales tax for a combined total of state and local taxes of 8 1/4%.

Funding

Taxes can either be general or dedicated. Typically, most taxes are general which means that they go into the taxing jurisdiction's general fund. Once in the general fund, these tax revenues fund the necessary operations of the government. However, sales taxes can be dedicated. This means that the tax is imposed for a specific purpose carved out from the general revenues collected by a government entity. An example of a dedicated sales tax is seen in the State of Texas where the state legislature passed a law allowing cities to increase the amount of sales tax they impose by ¼% over the otherwise state imposed cap, if those funds are dedicated to street maintenance and repair.

State of residency taxes

Citizens should definitely be concerned with what type of tax their state of residency imposes. First of all, acknowledgement of state imposed taxes is often necessary to properly comply. For example, ignorance of the existence of a state income tax could lead to a tax return not being filed. Secondly, the type of tax imposed can greatly affect an individual's economic situation. For example, someone who earns a high income but purchases relatively small amounts of goods and services will find themselves in a much better economic condition if they reside in a state that only imposes a sales tax. Also, national taxes become a relevant consideration. Until recently, only state income taxes were deductible on national income tax returns. Currently, both state income and sales taxes are deductible on national income tax returns, but not simultaneously. Therefore, striking the right balance could yield a substantial economic impact depending on an individual's particular circumstances.

Sin taxes

The most notable "sin" taxes are additional taxes, imposed at the state government level, on smoking, alcoholic beverages, and gambling activities. These "sin" taxes are actually a sub-category of excise taxes. Functionally, "sin" taxes operate much the same as sales taxes in that they are imposed at the moment of sale. However, unlike sales taxes, "sin" taxes are imposed only on the sale of specific products (e.g., alcoholic beverages) or certain activities (e.g., gambling). Also, unlike sales taxes or excise taxes in general, "sin" taxes are imposed with the stated purpose of dissuading the purchase of the taxed goods or undertaking the taxed activity. Due to the nature of the goods and activities taxed by "sin" taxes, they are often relatively easy to pass legislatively. For political reasons, even legislators who are opposed to taxes do not want to be viewed as permissive as to certain types of behavior.

Value added tax

The value added tax (VAT) is a revenue concept that has not been adopted in the United States. However, it is very prevalent in Europe and other parts of the world. VAT is similar to a sales tax with the main distinction being the timing and the taxed party. In a sales tax the consumer bears the responsibility for the tax at the time of sale. In a VAT, the creators, manufacturers, and/or retailers are responsible for the tax (however, it is naïve to think that these charges are not passed on to the consumer). Also, these taxes are imposed at various stages of the products life rather than just at the time of sale. Another distinction is, as the name implies, that the VAT imposes a tax on the amount of value added to the item at a particular stage in the item's development.

Intergovernmental contracts

Unlike taxes and user fees, intergovernmental contracts are very similar to how private companies raise revenue. For example, private companies generally contract with other companies (or governments) to provide goods and/or services for a fee. Intergovernmental contracts work in much the same way. Governments at the same (local to local) or different (state and local) levels can enter into agreements for the provision of services or to share services or facilities. States and local governments usually have specific provisions in their constitutions or charters allowing them to enter into intergovernmental contracts. These provisions will typically detail the requisite processes involved with entering into intergovernmental contracts as well. For example, some laws will provide that no outside bids are required prior to entering into intergovernmental contracts. It is possible that a particular intergovernmental contract does not involve raising revenue. Rather, some intergovernmental contracts outline the provision of overlapping services to citizens.

Intergovernmental grants

Intergovernmental grants are another method for government entities to attain funding. In the typical scenario, local government entities obtain grants from state governments and state governments obtain funds from the national government. However, local governments can obtain money directly from the national government as well. Obtaining funds from grants is different from raising revenue in the intergovernmental contracts context. The foremost distinction is that intergovernmental contracts involve a mutually beneficial agreement between two government entities (at the same or different levels of government) whereas an intergovernmental grant involves one entity giving funds to another. Despite the donative nature of intergovernmental grants, the granting government entity is often rewarded with some level of control over the recipient entity (or, at least, how the funds are utilized). There are two broad categories of intergovernmental grants: category grants and block grants.

<u>Intergovernmental category grants</u>
Intergovernmental category grants are a subcategory of intergovernmental grants. Category grants are grants that support a defined program area and the funds may only be spent only for a narrow purpose. Intergovernmental category grants can be further subdivided into formula grants and discretionary grants. These grants are often differentiated based on how they are awarded. Formula grants are noncompetitive and are awarded based on a predetermined formula. This formula is dictated by law or administrative regulation. These formulas are based on statistics that are relevant to the problem addressed by the grant. For example, if the grant is intended to help job training for unemployed citizens, then the formula might consider a requisite unemployment rate for an area to be eligible to receive the grant. Unlike formula grants, discretionary grants are awarded on a competitive basis. There is a formal application process where the applications are reviewed in light of the legislative and regulatory requirements and published selection criteria established for a program. The review process gives the granting entity discretion to determine which applications best address the program requirements and are, therefore, most worthy of funding.

Intergovernmental formula grant

There are many examples of intergovernmental formula grants at both the national and state level. Some intergovernmental formula grants at the national level include the Community Development Block Grants/State's Program (HUD), Crime Victim Assistance (DOJ), Employment Service (DOL), and National Motor Carrier Safety (DOT). Additionally, there is an intergovernmental formula grant for Cooperative Forestry Research administered by the United States Department of Agriculture. The stated goal of this national government program is "To encourage and assist the States in carrying on a program of State forestry research at State forestry schools, and to develop a trained pool of forest scientists capable of conducting needed forestry research." To ensure that the stated goals are attained, the grant carries restrictions. There are nine specific categories for which the grant money must be used. One such restriction is for "Reforestation and management of land for the production of crops of timber and other related products of the forest." The grant also specifies applicant eligibility, in this case all states and various United States possessions.

Intergovernmental discretionary grant

There are many types of intergovernmental discretionary grants. Due to the increased flexibility these grants provide the granting government entity, these grants tend to vary from year to year more so than formula grants. Additionally, intergovernmental discretionary grants are characterized by a trickle down

- 52 -

structure. For example, many states receive money for discretionary grants to local governments from the national government. Examples of intergovernmental discretionary grants at the national government level include: Rehabilitation Engineering Research Centers, Small Business Innovation Research Program, and Disability rehabilitation Research Projects (Note that this is a very small sample). Another specific example of a discretionary grant is the Teacher Incentive Fund. The purpose of this fund is to develop and implement performance based pay systems for teachers and principles in needy schools.* Eligible applicants for this grant include Local Education Agencies, Nonprofit Organizations, other organizations, and/or agencies, and State Education Agencies.

*Information taken from http://www.ed.gov/programs/teacherincentive/applicant.htm

Block grants

Block grants are one of the two types of intergovernmental grants (category grants being the other type). Where a category grant imposes fairly strict restraints on how the grant money can be spent, block grants contain relatively few restrictions on the grantee. An increase in the use of block grants by the United States government is seen as a step towards devolution of "New Federalism." In other words, block grants represent the shifting of power from the national government to the states. Typically, the national government will issue a block grant to a state or local government with a broad purpose specified. Within this context, the state or local government has the authority to determine how to best expend the funds to achieve this stated purpose. An example of a block grant includes the Local Law Enforcement Block Grant. All fifty states and the United States possession (e.g., Guam and Puerto Rico) are eligible for this national government grant. As the name indicates, the purpose of this block grant is to provide funds that enable local governments to tailor their own law enforcement projects given their particular crime problems. Within this broad goal are seven categories that limit how the funds may be spent. But allocation within this framework is completely up to the grantee.

Shared revenues

When discussing block grants (or any grants or contracts), the context is intergovernmental revenues. Block grants are a particular type of intergovernmental revenue source that typically benefits state and local governments. Perhaps the most distinguishing factor of block grants is the flexibility they provide the grantee in spending the revenue. Block grants are given to a state or local government with a general prescribed purpose attached to them. The recipient state or local government can then, within certain guidelines, allocate the funds in the best way they see fit to address the prescribed issue (e.g., crime reduction). The stereotypical shared revenue scenario involves money shared between a state and its local governments. Like block grants, shared revenues come with few restrictions to the recipient government. In fact, some states allocate a set portion of their tax revenues collected directly to local government's general funds (usually based on population). Once allocated to its general fund, the local government can use the revenue for any governmental purpose. This methodology of intergovernmental financing embodies the idea that localities are best equipped to handle their own issues.

Grantors level of accountability

Unlike intergovernmental contracts, where two independent government entities enter into a mutually beneficial arrangement (similar to private companies), grants and shared revenues lack a quid pro quo for the grantor. However, in the case of grants and shared revenues, the grantor of the funds does have expectations for the utilization of the revenue. More specifically, grantors expect a certain level of accountability from the recipient. Accountability in this context may include assurances that:
1. The money will be used for the purposes stated in the grant (these purposes can be very broad in the case of block grants and shared revenues);
2. The service recipients meet all of the eligibility requirements and are the types of service recipients meant to carry out the objective of the grant;
3. The grantee understands the difference between permitted and non-permitted costs, and takes steps to avoid non-permitted costs; and
4. The grantee meets any requirements for matching funds if such funds exist.

It is important to note that the current government trend towards greater reporting and transparency also applies in the grant context. For example, grantors are coming to expect greater reporting on the results of the grantees services provided with the granted funds. Additionally, grantors of grants that extend beyond a single budget period may request confirmation that the granted funds are utilized in such a way to last throughout the period of the grant. Finally, grantors may expect may expect that grantees comply with the overall goals of the grantor, even when not directly linked to the specific purpose of the grant issued. For example, if the Environmental Protection Agency where to issue a grant specifically for reforestation, they may implicitly require the grantee to carry out this mission in a way that doesn't damage other aspects of the environment.

Grantee in the grant process

Because the grantor-grantee relationship is akin to a giftor-giftee relationship, it is easy to understand that the grantor may have certain expectations tied to the transfer of funds to the recipient government entity. While, generally, recipient organizations are happy to receive funds from grants and shared revenues and happy to comply with any reasonable constraints on those funds, recipient organizations also have certain expectations of the grantor government entities. For instance, potential grantees want grant programs that utilize their normal operations. Grant recipients do not want the grant qualifications to require them to perform services that they are unaccustomed to providing. Note that this problem is often preempted by the fact that many grants are elective. Additionally, once a grant is issued, the recipient expects that the funds will be promptly transferred to facilitate the proper planning and organizing that is necessary to carry out the stated mission of the grant. Similarly, upon creating the infrastructure to accomplish the grant's goals, grantees need reasonable assurances that the funds will be available in the amounts and for the time periods specified in the grant. Any shortfall in this area could create overstaffing and other inefficiencies in the grantee's organization. Finally, grantees expect enough autonomy to accomplish the purpose set forth in the grant.

Government revenue

By far the most visible source of government revenue is taxation. This is because taxation affects every citizen in the United States, and every level of government is involved. Very broadly, there are three types of taxes (each with many subcategories): (1) income taxes, (2) wealth taxes, and (3) consumption taxes. Because of the numerous types of transactions and items subject to taxes, as well as the fact that all levels of government impose various taxes, they apply to nearly every citizen. As such, taxes are a very political issue. In theory, it would seem simple to address the many demands on government by raising taxes to increase revenue. However, the reality is that any tax increase no matter how seemingly justified, can carry negative political ramifications for those making such a proposition. Also, there are economic concerns. For example, increased monetary demands on the citizenry in the form of taxes means less money available for other types of spending. This can have negative implications on economic growth.

<u>Sources of government revenue</u>
License fees
In addition to taxes and intergovernmental revenues (contracts and grants/shared revenues) there are several other sources of revenue for governments. One such source is license fees. License fees are loosely defined as the cost charged by the government to attain its permission to undertake a specific activity. The activities that are subject to government license fees can very greatly. For instance, many business endeavors require government licensure. Examples of this are selling alcohol, operating adult businesses, commercial driving businesses, and veterinarians. Additionally, there are government licensing requirements for non-business pursuits. For example, licenses are required for hunting and for operating an automobile. For purposes of this discussion, the biggest governmental motive behind these fees is the revenue they provide. This revenue is attractive because it pays specifically for the costs associated with governmental responsibilities that directly stem from the activities themselves. For example, states require resources to oversee the conduct of attorneys within their jurisdiction and license fees provide these funds. Additionally, these fees are easier to legislate than broad taxes that affect citizens completely removed from the activities. Ignoring the revenue generated by license fees, it is important to note that these fees also allow the

government to regulate various activities without burdensome costs to the general citizenry.

User fees

User fees are similar to license fees in that they are very broad in scope. Additionally, user fees succeed in connecting the costs of providing specific services to revenues generated by providing those same services. As is the case with license fees, user fees limit the economic impact of providing certain services on non-users of that service. Other purposes of user fees are to provide for the expansion of government services (and/or related facilities) and absorb unexpected costs associated with these services. Although not always the case, user fees tend to be shorter term than licenses. Unlike license fees, user fees are not intended to regulate activities. However, user fees can be determined in such a way that encourages or discourages use of a particular government service. Another factor in determining user fees is the overall civic benefit provided by the service. If the civic benefit is low, then the user fee will be higher to pass along the majority of costs to the actual users. If the civic benefit is high, then the user fee will be lower requiring general tax revenue (or other revenue) to support the service.

Examples of government services that are subject to user fees abound. For example, at the local level of government many municipalities own and operate golf courses. Assume the town of Muni owns and operates a nine-hole golf course (course). Muni's city council determines that the best way to generate the revenue necessary to operate the course is through imposition of user fees on golfers who play the course. This is determined to be far more attractive that raising local property taxes or sales taxes because only users of the service (the course) are charged. Additionally, Muni is subject to periods of drought, and a user fee allows Muni to absorb any unexpected maintenance that may arise. Furthermore, Muni wishes to expand the nine-hole course into a full eighteen-hole course. This would attract more tourists from other towns and increase the profile of Muni in general. Imposition of a user fee facilitates this desire. Furthermore, adjusting the rate of user fees charged gives Muni some control over the use of the course. Finally, Muni determines that the overall civic benefit is relatively low. Therefore, the user fees are set so as to sustain the majority of the operating costs of the course.

Lotteries

Another source is lotteries. While all forms of government revenue are subject to some controversy, this is especially the case with lotteries. Lotteries are often criticized and opposed because they are a form of gambling and they allegedly take advantage of the poor and elderly (constituents most likely to require some form of government assistance in the first place). There are state run lotteries in forty-two states as well as Puerto Rico and the District of Columbia. (Information taken from http://www.lotteryusa.com.) Despite the controversy surrounding lotteries, many legislators find them easier to implement than tax increases. Additionally, lotteries are attractive because they can raise large amounts of revenue very quickly. Often lottery revenue is tied to specific programs. For example, the Texas State Lottery applies twenty-seven percent of its revenue to education. (Information taken from http://www.txlottery.org/faq/moneygoes.cfm.)

Legalized gambling
As is the case with lotteries, legalized gambling is subject to a great deal of controversy and is strongly opposed by many citizens. In addition to the moral implications, many citizens fear that gambling invites other negative social problems into their jurisdiction (e.g., increased crime). Despite these concerns, legalized gambling is growing as a governmental revenue source. The term "legalized gambling" is a very broad term that encompasses many forms of gambling. For example, casino gambling, dog track betting and horse track betting are all forms of gambling. Some states allow only limited types of gambling (e.g., Louisiana, at one time, only permitted riverboat casinos).

*Note that there are other minor forms of governmental revenue including: returns on investments, payments of fines, fees for the exploitation of natural resources, monies generated from sales of government assets (typically at auction), etc.

Government lotteries vs. legalized gambling
A key distinction between legalized gambling and lotteries is there operation at the government level. Lotteries are typically operated by the government itself through a specific government entity. However, with regards to legalized gambling, governments (typically state governments) award a license to a private gambling company who runs the gambling operation. Therefore, the government is merely a regulator who shares in the profits of the gambling operation. Many states now permit some form of legalized gambling. For example, the state of Pennsylvania legalized slot machine gambling in 2004. The first slots casino opened in 2006. The state law that legalized slot gambling in Pennsylvania also dictates the uses of the revenues. The revenues are to be applied to reduce state property taxes, reduce Philadelphia's wage tax, increase horse-racing payouts, and fund rebates of rental expenses for senior citizens.

Government debt

Government debt can take many forms. For example, government entities can issue bonds, notes, and certificates of participation. However, just as with individuals or private entities, government entities are expected and obligated to repay their debts. If there is a failure to repay debts, government entities can be subjected to bankruptcy proceedings. It is rare for government entities to enter bankruptcy, but not unprecedented. For example, in 1994 Orange County, California entered Chapter 9 bankruptcy. This is considered to be the largest municipal bankruptcy in United States history. Ironically, Orange County, California is an extremely affluent area. Apparently, the cause of Orange County's bankruptcy was not expenses exceeding revenues, but rather the mismanagement of billions of dollars in an investment fund.

Purposes of government debt

At the national level of government, debt funds are utilized for capital improvements as well as for day-to-day operations. At the state and local level, debt funds are predominantly utilized to cover infrastructure expenditures. Most state and local governments do not bring in enough revenue to cover the costs of expensive capital projects (e.g., building schools and renovating existing structures). Therefore, state and local governments will typically enter into long-term debt financing to pay for such expenditures. Utilizing debt allows for states and local governments to defer the costs of large capital projects over longer periods of time. This allows other revenues to pay for the various projects over its life. Additionally, financing large projects with long-term debt ensures that the citizens who enjoy the use of the improvement will be the one paying for it (primarily through their property, sales, and/or income taxes). Another purpose of government debt is to provide short-term financing when future funds are probable. This financing can occur when proceeds are expected from taxes, other revenues, bonds, or grants. Finally, governments will incur new debts at favorable rates to pay of older debts that have less favorable terms. This process is referred to as refunding.

Levels of government in respect to acquiring debt

Different levels of government are limited in how they can utilize debt. The United States government is given broad authority under the United States Constitution to fund current operating expenses as well as capital improvements. Conversely, most state constitutions provide that debt funds may only be utilized for capital improvements. For those states/localities that do allow funds acquired through the issuance of debt to pay for operating expenses, there are typically strict requirements that dictate such debts shall be repaid within a one year period. The obvious intent of such tight controls at the state and local level is to avoid large debt balances. Because the national government does not have such controls, the national government is currently in debt. At the time of this writing, the amount of the national debt exceeds $8 trillion.

Advanced refunding

In very broad terms, advanced refunding is a specific purpose for a government to elect to incur debt. Governments, like private citizens and private businesses prefer to borrow money at the lowest rates possible. Therefore, governments sometimes assume new debt to retire older debt when the terms are more favorable on the newer debt. This is analogous to a private citizen refinancing his/her home mortgage at a lower interest rate. Advanced refunding is a specific type of governmental refinance. In the case of an advanced refunding the government entity issues a new debt issue at a lower rate than current outstanding debt issue. These new debt issues are issued prior to the first call date of the old debt issues. While awaiting the first call date on the old debt issue, the proceeds from the new debt issue are escrowed and eventually pay for the old debt issue.

<u>Limitations</u>
Because of the potential financial dangers involved with acquiring debt, government borrowing is subject to many limitations. Furthermore, all levels of government are subject to limitations. The United States Congress sets the limits for the national government and changes this limit on occasion. States borrowing limits are determined by their constitution, statutes, or both. Similarly, local governments are subject to the Constitution and laws of their state as well as any further restrictive local ordinances. The subject of the limitation is also variable. Some jurisdictions limit debt by imposing a stop on the amount of outstanding debt. Other jurisdictions base their limitations on an amount that can be used to service the debt. Furthermore, the amounts of the limitations can be expressed in different terms. For example, some states express their debt limitations as specific dollar amounts while others express their debt limitations as percentages of some other value.

Incurring debt

Incurring debt is a serious consideration for any government entity. There is very real risk associated with issuing debt. For example, government entities are subject to bankruptcy proceedings in the event they cannot meet their repayment requirements. Additionally, debt is not always a preferable method of acquiring funds because of the many limitations imposed on government entities that go into debt. Finally, there are other considerations that must be addressed before a government entity elects debt as a financing option. The most obvious of these considerations is determining if the funds sought can be better acquired from other (non-debt) sources. These other sources may include tax revenues, grants/revenue shares, or other sources. Also, because of the risk of bankruptcy, government entities must seriously consider their ability to shoulder the financial burden of repaying the debt. Implicit in the consideration of debt repayment is proper evaluation of the citizens who will ultimately repay the debt. If a small jurisdiction is overly aggressive in its debt financing, it risks overtaxing and under serving its constituents.

Government debt financing

Because of the risks and other negatives that accompany debt financing, some jurisdictions avoid debt altogether. This may prove the ideal situation for specific jurisdictions; however, avoidance of debt also has negative aspects. For example, if all capital improvements are paid for up front with current (or surplus from prior years) tax revenues, then future citizens will enjoy the use of such improvements without having paid for them. Also, using current revenues to pay for projects is lees attractive in an inflationary market. At times of inflation, debt is favorable because the payment obligation of the government on the debt issue is fixed while its other revenue can be invested elsewhere to take advantage of the inflated interest rates. Similarly, if a government entity uses all or most of its current revenue for current projects, the entity may be poorly situated for any emergency or

- 59 -

unexpected monetary need. Such a situation could require the government entity to borrow at less favorable terms because the exigent conditions. Finally, avoidance of debt may lead to underdeveloped infrastructures in growing jurisdictions. In a rapidly growing area, the need for capital improvements increases dramatically while the collection of revenues from the growth lags behind. Responsible debt issuances allow governments to make the needed improvements and pay for them in the future with the increased revenue from the growth.

Debt policy
When a government entity decides to enter into debt financing, a debt policy should be formalized. Because of the hazardous nature of debt financing, a well thought out debt policy can avoid many of the pitfalls inherent in the borrowing process. For example, a good debt policy establishes checks on the amount of debt acquired. This is important for two reasons:
- government entities are typically limited (by constitutional provision or statute) as to how much debt they are permitted to issue, and
- the amount of debt a government entity takes on should always be monitored in relation to its ability to pay (e.g., expected revenues).

Additionally, a competent debt policy will track the various debts based on the type of debt and, particularly, based on maturity date. Ensuring that all of the government entity's debts do not mature at the same time is critical to ensuring that the entity will be able to meet its obligations.

Example of a formal debt policy
The following is the formal debt policy for the City of Champagne, Illinois.
CITY OF CHAMPAIGN DEBT POLICIES*
I. PURPOSE AND GENERAL POLICIES
A. Purpose. This policy establishes guidelines for use of debt financing that will allow the City to minimize financing costs and retain or improve its Aa-1 bond rating from Moody's Investors Services (or an equivalent rating from a similar firm.)
B. Conditions under which the City may consider use of debt financing.
   The City may consider the use of debt financing when all of the following conditions apply:
   - for one-time capital improvement projects and unusual equipment purchases,
   - when the project's useful life, or the projected service life of the equipment, will exceed the term of financing, and
   - when the City has identified revenues sufficient to service the debt, either from existing revenues or increased taxes or fees. The City will not use debt for any recurring purpose such as current operating and infrastructure maintenance expenditures, nor will the City use short-term debt, unless under exigent circumstances.

Bonds

From the standpoint of the government entity issuing them, bonds represent a debt obligation to pay a set amount of money at a predetermined date to the holder of the bond. This set amount of money may be referred to as the bonds principal, par value, or face value. The date upon which the government entity must pay the bond holder the principal of the bond is commonly known as the maturity date. In addition to paying the bond holder the principal amount, bonds also require the issuer to pay interest. This interest, also referred to as the coupon rate, is usually expressed as an annual percentage of the par value of the bond. Note that there are some bonds that do not pay interest. These are known as zero coupon bonds. Broadly speaking, there are two types of government bonds: (1) general obligation bonds and (2) revenue bonds.
Note that private corporations also issue bonds.

General obligation bonds
A general obligation bond is a bond that is backed by all sources of credit and revenue of the government entity issuing the bonds. With general obligation bonds, no particular assets are used as collateral for the repayment obligation. Instead, repayment of general obligation bonds comes from government revenue acquired through taxation or other sources of revenue. One advantage general obligation bonds offer to the issuing government entity is lower interest rates (compared to revenue bonds). The reason that government entities can pay so little interest on general obligation bonds is due to the fact that all sources of credit and revenue of the government entity are available for repayment of the bond. As a result, general obligation bonds are considered very safe (unless, of course, the issuing government entity is known to be in serious financial difficulty). On the downside, general obligation bonds often must be voter approved before they can be issued. Additionally, general obligations are frequently counted against debt limits imposed on the government entity by constitution or statute. Keep in mind that general obligation bonds are predominantly utilized to fund projects that benefit the community as a whole.

Revenue bonds
Revenue bonds are the most prevalent type of government bond issued. Revenue bonds are distinguished from general obligation bonds in that the former are secured by a particular source of revenue. In the generic case, revenue bonds are issued to fund the expenses of a particular project that will generate revenue upon its completion. This revenue is the collateral for the revenue bond. However, revenue bonds may also be collateralized by a dedicated tax. In either case, underlying goal in using revenue bonds is to match those that will benefit from the project with those that will ultimately pay for the project. Because revenue bonds offer bond holders less collateral (compared to general obligation bonds), they are considered riskier investments. As such, government entities usually must offer higher interest rates (or coupon rates) to holders to make the bonds attractive in the open market. Due to the varying nature of the projects financed by revenue

- 61 -

bonds, these bonds tend to vary greatly from case to case. Each revenue bond usually contains many covenants that outline the details of the bond.

Example
There are numerous types of revenue bonds used in virtually every jurisdiction in the United States. Industrial revenue bonds are one particular type of revenue bond that is used in many jurisdictions. The State of Texas Industrial Revenue Bond Program is indicative of many programs utilized throughout the United States. Industrial revenue bonds are intended to provide financing with favorable terms to finance the completion of eligible industrial or manufacturing projects. Prior to issuing these bonds, a particular Texas government entity forms an industrial development corporation. This industrial development corporation actually issues the industrial revenue bonds once a bond resolution is passed. This resolution must then be passed by another resolution of the government entity that created the industrial development corporation. The industrial revenue bonds are not a debt or an obligation of the government entity, the industrial development corporation, or the State of Texas.

Repayment of revenue bonds
Revenue bonds differ from general obligation bonds in that their repayment derives from a specific source as opposed to the general resources of the issuing government entity. This specific source of repayment is the revenue generated from the project funded by the bond issuance. The revenue generated from the project pays both the interest and the face value of the revenue bond at maturity. Because revenue from such projects can be unpredictable and uneven (especially in earlier years), government entities issuing revenue bonds will often establish a fund to cover payment obligations when the project's revenues are insufficient. This unpredictable nature of project revenues is the reason that revenue bonds typically require payment of a higher interest rate that general obligation bonds.

Special assessment bonds
Special assessment bonds are a type of revenue bond. A general obligation bond is secured by the full faith and credit of the issuing government entity. Revenue bonds, however, are backed by the revenue generated from a specific revenue source. This source can be the revenue generated by the project funded by the bonds (e.g., a toll road) or the revenue can come from special assessments made on citizens who directly benefit from the project. These latter situations are special assessment bonds. For example, a government entity may need funds to repave a specific neighborhood's roads. It wouldn't be particularly equitable to charge the general tax base with the costs of these improvements because only a few citizens benefit. Additionally, the project itself will not generate its own revenue that can support the costs. In these cases, special assessment bonds are appropriate because the issuance of the bonds provide the government entity with the necessary revenue to complete the project. Because the repayment of these bonds will come from assessments made on the benefiting citizens, equity is achieved.

Term bonds

Term bonds are a group of bonds that are set to mature in the same year. Term bonds, which are general obligation bonds, can represent a large obligation on the part of the issuing government entity. As a result, it is common for issuing government entities to contribute to a sinking fund over the life of the bonds. A sinking fund is a fund designed to gradually (usually over the term of the obligation) accumulate the requisite funds necessary to meet a future obligation. The benefit of this to the government entity is that it allows them to spread out their repayment obligation. This is especially beneficial considering most term bonds mature long after their issue (e.g., 25-30 years). It is important to note that term bonds can be retired prior to maturity.

Serial bonds

Serial bonds can be thought of as the exact opposite of term bonds. Where term bonds are a group of bonds set to mature in the same year, serial bonds are a group of bonds issued simultaneously with different maturity dates. Serial bonds usually mature every year (or twice a year) over a set period of time after issuance. Serial bonds (also referred to as installment bonds) are typically used to fund projects that will yield a regular, level, or predictable income stream. The advantage of a serial bond issue over a term bond issue from the issuing government entity's perspective is that there is no large obligation that is set to mature all at once. However, serial bond issues do begin to mature earlier than term bond issues. Therefore, they represent a more impending obligation than term bond issues. However, because a sinking bond is established for most term bond issues, the functional differences among these types of bond issues are not that great.

Covenants

Covenants apply to specific government bond issuances. These covenants are restrictions in the sense that they represent a promise from the issuer to the purchaser. These promises are formally memorialized as a contractual provision of the bond itself. Covenants can be either positive or negative. Positive covenants require the issuing government to do certain things. Negative covenants require the issuing government to avoid doing certain things. Often, both types of covenants are present in a single bond issuance. Covenants are taken very seriously as any violation of a bond's covenants can yield a technical default. As a result, governments oversee compliance with bond covenants vehemently. For example, Sunnyvale, California's Finance Department lists meeting all bond covenants as one of its primary missions.* Specific bond covenants include establishing a pay-off date (maturity date), setting the interest that will be paid to bond purchasers, setting a payment schedule for the payment of interest, and identifying funds that will shoulder the burden of the repayments. Covenants may also require government entities to create funds to gather money for eventual repayment of the obligation (aka, sinking funds).

*Information taken from http://sunnyvale.ca.gov/Departments/Finance/Treasury/

<u>Example at the state level</u>
The State of Montana has a statute that lists the scope of covenants that may be entered into in conjunction with bond issuances. This statute is located in Montana Code Annotated (1997) 60-11-1106. It states:
The department may enter into covenants with the bondholders by resolution, trust indenture, or other appropriate security instrument to enhance the marketability of the bonds. These covenants may relate to: the purpose to which the bond proceeds are to be applied; the use and disposition of the revenue of a project to which the bond proceeds are to be applied; the issuance of additional bonds to be paid from revenue of a project to which the bond proceeds are to be applied; the insurance to be carried on a project to which bond proceeds are to be applied; the accounting procedures and auditing powers related to a project; the terms and conditions upon which the bondholders are entitled to have a receiver appointed to operate a project to which bond proceeds are to be applied; the maintenance of a required capital reserve; the granting of a mortgage and security interest in the project and other properties of the borrower to secure the bonds; such other matters as the department considers customary and appropriate to secure the bonds. Note that this provision permissive (rather than limiting) in that it permits the state to enter into covenants that increase the marketability of the bonds. However, covenants that benefit purchasers no doubt limit the issuer

Retiring bonds

First, and foremost, government entities want to retire their issued bonds because this relieves them of their payment obligations. Stated another way, since bonds represent debt of the government entity, their retirement means the government entity is no longer in debt (with regards to that particular indebtedness). Additionally, there can be financial reasons supporting a government entity's desire to retire debt that extent beyond mere debt relief. Most notably, government entities can greatly benefit from restructuring their debt to take advantage of market conditions that are more favorable than those that existed at the date of the original issuance. For example, assume a government entity issued bonds (in other words, borrowed money) at a time of high interest rates and those interest rates subsequently dropped. Restructuring their debt would allow the issuing government entity to replace their old bonds (which obligate the government entity to pay high interest rates to bond holders) with new bonds (which obligate the government entity to pay lower interest rates to bond holders).

In addition to compelling economic reasons for retiring bonds, government entities may also realize non-economic benefits as well. For example, governments at the state and local level are usually subject to strict limitations on how much debt they can carry as well as the purposes for which they can carry debt. Therefore, if a government entity has reached the maximum level of debt that it can carry then management loses debt as a financing option for the completion of needed projects. Additionally, bond issues contain covenants. Sometimes these covenants require more than just specification of an interest rate and maturity date. Bond covenants may require the issuing government entity to do (or not do) specific things that are burdensome to the entity. For example, bond covenants may require the filing of additional reports. Retirement of the bond subject to these covenants also eliminates the covenants themselves. Often, government entities want to retire bonds containing burdensome covenants with bonds subject to less burdensome covenants. Careful analysis of all of the costs involved is required because there are many cost inefficiencies in bond issuances. Additionally, some bonds are subject to legal limitations regarding retirement prior to maturity.

Government issued warrants

Government issued warrants are similar to post-dated checks. Governments will occasionally issue checks that they are unable to fully cover at the time they issue the check. Therefore, these checks will pay interest to the recipient. These instruments are referred to as warrants. Warrants may be used by government entities to provide current funds for any number of obligations, including paying bond obligations. Warrants are not always an ideal way for government entities to meet the bond obligations. This is true because warrants simple give rise to new obligations for the government entity. As a result of this new obligation, some jurisdictions are required by law to establish funds to repay their warrant obligations. For example, the State of Arizona requires the establishment of such a fund. In fact, Arizona requires that "all monies that would otherwise be paid into the state general fund, except for amounts sufficient to pay the salaries of constitutional officers of this state, shall be deposited into the treasurer's warrant note redemption fund."

Government notes

Similar to government bonds, government notes are a form of debt financing. The main distinction separating government notes from government bonds is their duration. Government bonds tend to be long-term. In fact, most government bonds mature twenty-five to thirty years after their date of issue. However, government notes tend to be much shorter in term. Because of this shorter maturity period, government notes often repay both the principal and interest on the maturity date. Additionally, the shorter term of government notes requires different planning from a financial management perspective. For example, short-term government notes would not work well as a financing option for a long-term project. Instead, government notes are generally issued only when revenue is expected in the immediate future and there is only a small gap of time where debt financing is necessary. Two examples of these government notes are bond anticipation notes and revenue anticipation notes. Because government notes are short-term and very low risk, they tend to offer investors lower interest rates than bonds.

Example
The town on Northumberland, New York issued a bond anticipation note on October 13, 2004. The purpose of this issuance was to raise funds to purchase a dump truck

with a snow plow. The amount of the bond anticipation note was eighty thousand dollars. On October 12, 2005, the Town Board of Northumberland paid off twenty thousand of the original eighty thousand dollar note and issued a sixty thousand dollar bond anticipation renewal note for the remaining sixty thousand dollar obligation. The Town Board agreed to pay off twenty thousand dollars of the remaining sixty thousand dollar bond anticipation renewal note on October 11, 2006 with the remaining forty thousand dollars to mature on or before October 10, 2007. This vote passed unanimously (five to zero) on October 2, 2006 at a special Town Board meeting.

Lease-purchases

Lease-purchases are a vehicle for government entities to acquire both personal and real property without incurring debt and, in many cases, not requiring voter approval. Lease-purchases are categorized as a long-term financing option for government entities in that they allow the purchase of needed property over an extended (sometimes the life of the asset) period of time. The government entity's obligation under a lease-purchase contract is less secured in that the lease-purchase contract is contingent upon the annual appropriation of funds during the life of the contract. The timing of passage of title to the government entity is variable and is part of the negotiation process. Detractors note that lease-purchase agreements usually cost the government more in terms of interest paid for drawing out the purchase of the subject asset that if the asset were purchased with traditional government debt acquired through issuing bonds. However, this disparity can often be made up for in efficiency costs because lease-purchase agreements require little in the way of government officials' time, legal expense, and the uncertainty of voter involvement.

Certificates of participation

Certificates of participation are a bi-product of a government entity entering into a lease transaction. Typically, a government entity will seek to lease some property (personal or real). In the case of a large project, this lease is underwritten by a financial institution that provides the funds to an authority of the government entity (or a third party) that builds the project and then leases it to the government entity. This loan is backed only by the value of the asset, not the revenue of the government entity (as is the case with bonds). The financial institution then issues certificates of participation to investors allowing them to share in the lease revenues achieved as the government entity pays its lease. Sometimes, the full payment of the lease results in the government entity taking title to the property. This is the case in a lease-purchase agreement. From the government's standpoint, certificates of participation are valuable in that they allow for necessary projects to be undertaken without voter approval and without booking more debt (which is subject to strict limitations). From the investor's viewpoint, certificates of participation allow the investor to share in the revenue generated by the lease payments.

There are many detractors of certificates of participation. Broadly speaking, certificates of participation are attacked as allowing government entities to subvert the voter approval process and take what functionally equates to debt without having to adhere to the formalities and safeguards that accompany a stereotypical debt borrowing. For example, at the local level of government, some government entities have sought voter approval for the issuance of bonds (assumption of debt) to complete projects (prison construction to golf course improvements). Upon failing to receive voter approval, the government entity then creates a special agency solely for the purpose of issuing certificates of participation. These certificates of participation are then sold to the public and the funds generated from the sale are used to build the project. While the special agency, and not the government entity, is specifically liable for the repayment on the certificates of participation, any failure to repay will severely impact the government entity's bond rating. Therefore, the government entity is, in reality, concerned with the payment on the certificates of participation. Further, projects undertaken in this manner tend to be less efficient to the government than straight bond issues because certificates of participation are viewed as riskier investments and, therefore, demand higher interest payments.

Credit-rating agencies

Credit-rating agencies are organizations that rate the creditworthiness of a debt issuance. This is determined by analyzing the ability of the issuing party's ability to repay the debt that is being issued. A credit-rating agency greatly impacts a government entity's financing options because credit ratings (or scores) determine the cost of borrowing money for the government entity. For example, if a government entity receives a poor credit rating, it is forced to pay much higher interest on its debt obligations than a government entity that receives a high or good credit rating. In some cases, the higher interest that is demanded of poor credit scoring government entity may negate debt as a revenue source. It should be noted that credit-rating agencies also evaluate private companies' and private citizens' creditworthiness. The three major credit-rating agencies for government entities are Standard & Poor's, Moody's Investor Service, and Fitch Ratings.

Rating factors

Before a government entity issues bonds or other debt, a credit-rating agency will evaluate the issuance and assign it a rating or score. Typically, the interest rate offered to investors (e.g., bond purchasers) is based in large part on this score. The higher the rating of the issuing government entity and the debt itself, the lower the interest rate the government entity will have to pay investors. This is due to the correlation between credit rating and investment risk. Some of the factors analyzed in rating a debt issuance include:
- Specifics of the debt being issued. This can include the duration of the instrument, how the funds are to be used by the government entity, the funds designated for debt repayment, etc.

- Government entity's ability to service the debt. Implicit in this category is the consideration of the government entity's other debts as well as any anticipated future debts and how effectively the government entity can support the new issue in light of this other debt.
- Economic forecast as it will apply to the specific government entity.
- The financial condition of the government entity.
- The management practices of the government entity. This focuses on the competence of those in charge of the government entity.

<u>Specific ratings</u>

For government debt ratings there are three major credit-rating agencies. They are Standard & Poor's, Moody's Investor Service, and Fitch Ratings. Below is a chart the lists each rating code and its corresponding grade and risk level. Keep in mind that the higher the rating, the lower the risk and the lower the interest rate a government entity will have to pay to sell its debt issuance in the open market. Also note that some types of investors are prohibited from investing in debt issues below certain rating.

<u>Moody's: Aaa S&P/Fitch: AAA</u>
Grade: Investment Risk: Lowest Risk/Highest Quality
<u>Moody's: Aa S&P/Fitch: AA</u>
Grade: Investment Risk: Low Risk/High Quality
<u>Moody's: A S&P/Fitch: A</u>
Grade: Investment Risk: Some Risk/Strong
<u>Moody's: Baa S&P/Fitch: BBB</u>
Grade: Investment Risk: Risk is Present/Medium Grade
<u>Moody's: Ba, B S&P/Fitch: BB, B</u>
Grade: Junk Risk: High Risk/Speculative
<u>Moody's: Caa/Ca/C S&P/Fitch: CCC/CC/C</u>
Grade: Junk Risk: Very High Risk/Highly Speculative
<u>Moody's: C S&P/Fitch: D</u>
Grade: Junk Risk: Risk Realized/In Default

Special-purpose governments

Special-purpose governments are governments or government entities created by a general-purpose government for a specific purpose or several related purposes. Despite their narrow focus and, sometimes, temporary existence, special-purpose governments require funding and face the same difficulties in financing their operations that general-purpose governments face. In order to achieve their goals, special-purpose governments may utilize appropriations, user fees, taxes, bond issues to obtain funds. In this regard, special-purpose governments raise funds in the same manner that general-purpose governments do. However, special-purpose governments are somewhat more flexible than general-purpose governments in that special-purpose governments may earn interest on investments in other entities.

Appropriations

An appropriation occurs when money is designated for a specific purpose. Therefore, it makes sense that special-purpose governments, which are created by general-purpose governments for a specific purpose or set of related purposes, receive appropriations. For an appropriation to occur, it must comply with the United States Constitution. Specifically, Article 1 of the United States Constitution requires that appropriations from the Treasury be made by specific law. Therefore, if Congress identifies a specific need that it wishes to address and also identifies a special-purpose government(s) that Congress believes can address the need, an appropriation can be passed that will provide the special-purpose government with funds. Examples of needs that are addressed through appropriations are education, park service (national, state, and local), and poverty. While appropriations are direct in that they come straight from Congress, special-purpose governments can receive appropriated funds indirectly. This occurs when the general-purpose government that created the special-purpose government receives appropriated funds from Congress and subsequently transitions the funds (or a portion thereof) to the special-purpose government.

User fees

User fees are similar to license fees in that they are very broad in scope. Additionally, user fees succeed in connecting the costs of providing specific services to revenues generated by providing those same services. User fees limit the economic impact of providing certain services on non-users of that service. Other purposes of user fees are to provide for the expansion of government services (and/or related facilities) and absorb unexpected costs associated with these services. Although not always the case, user fees tend to be shorter term than licenses. Unlike license fees, user fees are not intended to regulate activities. However, user fees can be determined in such a way that encourages or discourages use of a particular government service. Another factor in determining user fees is the overall civic benefit provided by the service. If the civic benefit is low, then the user fee will be higher to pass along the majority of costs to the actual users. If the civic benefit is high, then the user fee will be lower requiring general tax revenue (or other revenue) to support the service. User fees are very appropriate for special-purpose governments because user fees are charged for a specific service or use and special-purpose governments typically conduct very specific operations. In some case, special-purpose governments can be completely funded by user fees.

Taxes

Some special-purpose governments collect revenue from taxes. This process is similar to the taxes collected by general-purpose governments except that special-purpose governments are far more limited in their taxing authority. In the typical scenario, a special-purpose government will assess taxes on property owned by businesses and citizens within its jurisdiction. These taxes are meant to tax those that benefit the most from the services provided by the special-purpose government. A common problem that arises in the context of special-purpose government taxation is double taxation. This occurs when the jurisdictions of more than one special-purpose government overlap. When this happens, sometimes services and taxes are duplicated on the affected property owners. To address this problem, general-purpose governments often have specific statutes to determine which special-purpose government has jurisdiction. For example, the State of Washington has a law that states that where such duplication exists, the first jurisdiction to include the property wins.

Bond issues
Bond issues allow government entities to acquire funds by incurring debt. At the national level of government, debt funds are utilized for capital improvements as well as for day-to-day operations. At the state and local level, debt funds are predominantly utilized to cover infrastructure expenditures. Most state and local governments do not bring in enough revenue to cover the costs of expensive capital projects (e.g., building schools and renovating existing structures). Therefore, state and local governments will typically enter into long-term debt financing to pay for such expenditures. Utilizing debt allows for states and local governments to defer the costs of large capital projects over longer periods of time. This allows other revenues to pay for the various projects over its life. Additionally, financing large projects with long-term debt ensures that the citizens who enjoy the use of the improvement will be the one paying for it (primarily through their property, sales, and/or income taxes). Another purpose of government debt is to provide short-term financing when future funds are probable. This financing can occur when proceeds are expected from taxes, other revenues, bonds, or grants. Special-purpose governments obtain their authority to issue bonds from the law that created the special-purpose government. It should be noted that bond issues at any level of government are subject to strict limitations. However, even greater oversight occurs when a special-purpose government issues debt.

Financing structure example
There are countless special-purpose governments throughout the United States. These entities range from parks and recreational departments to school districts to police departments. One specific example of a special-purpose government is Austin Community College in Austin, Texas. Austin Community College, like other special-purpose governments receives money from various sources. Specifically, for the 2001 fiscal year Austin Community College received the following percentage of funds from the following sources:
- 37% of funds from state appropriations
- 29% of funds from tuition and fees
- 17% of funds from property taxes
- 9% of funds from contracts and grants
- 8% from other sources.

Constitutions and charters

There are many reasons why governments need to borrow funds. For instance, in times where revenues are down (e.g., during a sluggish economy) governments may require funds to remain operational. Even when government revenues are high there can be special unforeseen circumstances that justify the issuance of government debt instruments (e.g., times of war, natural disasters, etc.). However, the government's ability to issue debt instruments is not unchecked. Legal limitations curtail government borrowing in a variety of ways. For instance, governments are limited to borrowing money for certain reasons (e.g., building infrastructure). Additionally, laws dictate how long government debt instruments can remain outstanding. Similarly, governments of all levels are limited as to how much money they can borrow. These limits are expressed in several ways. The national government has a limit on the absolute value of the debt it can incur, while states may set a limitation on debt as it relates to the overall budget. Finally, government borrowing is held in check by citizens. Typically, government can only borrow after a favorable vote from the affected citizens (e.g., referendum).

Limiting government spending

Account structures limit government spending by dictating the expenditure of funds based on program or object class. Where the spending is limited by program, this means that only the pursuit of certain enumerated goals or purposes justify a monetary expenditure. For example, government spending is limited by program where the budget calls for money to be spent on elder care facilities.

Where the spending is limited by object class, this means that appropriated funds can only be spent on certain goods or services. For example, a budget that dictates certain amounts can only be spent on office furniture is limited by object class. Note that object class is also known as a line-item.

Account structures assist in evaluating the success of a particular program, but are criticized as lacking flexibility in certain instances. For example, where spending is limited by object class, if a shortfall exists as to spending for a particular good or service, it is difficult to get the approval to reallocate more funds to eliminate the shortfall.

Account structures designate funds as either special or general. General funds can be spent for any authorized purp0ose, while special funds may only be spent for clearly identified purposes.

Earmarking

Account structures generally limit how the government can spend money appropriated to it. One such limitation is the designation of funds as special funds. This designation means that the funds may only be spent for clearly identified purposes. Government revenues that are "earmarked" are a type of special funds. Earmarked funds are not only limited in how they can be spent, they are also specifically identified by how they are generated. Furthermore, their collection and expenditure is often connected by policy considerations. For example, a government could collect revenues from the operation of toll roads and earmark these funds for a special fund that spends money on road improvement projects. Note that earmarking, like other spending limitations, reduces control that governments have over how revenues may be spent.

Spending authority

For reference, this assumes that money has already been appropriated for use by specific government agencies and their components. Spending plans, apportionments, and allotments exist to make sure that the appropriated funds are utilized for the correct purposes and at a correct rate so that the funds aren't exhausted before the end of the budget period (one year at the national level).

Agencies (typically executive branch) may be required to submit a spending plan which details how the agency will use the funds. These spending plans are utilized to ensure that the actual spending by the agency is proper. Apportionments refer to the conveyance of budget authority from the government's central management agency (Office of Management and Budget at the national level) to the specific agency that has been (or will be) appropriated funds. Once the agency receives its apportionment, it allots spending authority to its various components to achieve its purpose. Apportionments and allotments are usually disbursed every quarter to ensure that the appropriated funds last for the entire budget year and to allow for any reallocation of funds.

Note that the terminology may vary at the state and local levels, but this general path is followed.

Government accounting

Government accounting utilizes fund accounting. Under this approach, separate self-balancing accounts are used to manage government resources that are to be spent for specific purposes. Unlike private-sector accounting where revenue is recognized when earned and expenses when they are incurred, government accounting is recognized when funds are available to liquidate liabilities within the current accounting period and expenses are recognized when current demand is made on resources. There are two main reasons why private and public sector accounting differ: (1) the private sector is profit driven while the public sector is not and (2) the private-sector budget is just a financial planning instrument while in the public sector, compliance with the budget is mandatory. Therefore, government accounting is another way or imposing fiscal accountability on those who spend public funds.

Government auditing

Government auditing is the process by which budgetary (and other) operations conducted by government entities are evaluated based on clearly identified criteria. Government auditing may be conducted from within the government itself (internal audit) or by third parties outside of government (external audit). Government audits are intended to identify and correct any procedural mistakes as well as uncover fraud or intentional wrongdoing.

Note that the United States (and state and local) government does audit individuals for tax compliance. However this practice is conducted by the Internal Revenue Service (under the Department of Treasury) and is not referred to as government auditing.

Public accountability

Authorities U.S. citizens possess

The indirect and direct authorities U.S. citizens possess over the government are:
- Indirect: U.S. citizens can vote on and elect officials to establish and administer policy (e.g., the chief executive and members of Congress).
- Direct: State and local governments, through their constitutions and charters, may be subject to the following methods of direct action by their citizens; (1) Initiative: Process where state and local citizens address a specific concern with a specific cure. Initiatives are voted for or against by the citizens of the jurisdiction. While viewed as a direct authority over government, initiatives can be direct or indirect. In the case of a direct initiative, a measure is put directly to a vote after being submitted by a petition. An indirect initiative is where a measure is first referred to the legislature, and then only put to a popular vote if not enacted by the legislature. An example of a direct initiative is Washington State's initiative number 884 where citizens voted on a proposal to increase the sales tax by one percent to establish an education trust fund.
- Referendum: These require that certain actions taken by the legislature be subjected to voter approval before these actions become state or local law. This typically refers to a popular vote to overturn legislation already passed at the state or local levels.
- Recall: The recall is similar to the concept of impeachment. This power allows citizens to terminate the service of elected officials. This form of direct government is less prevalent than the other two because it is prohibited in thirty-two out of fifty states. An example of the use of recall is North Dakota's recall of Governor Lynn J. Frazier in 1921.

Government accountability

Government accountability is one of, if not the, main foundational blocks of a democratic government. Obviously, the United States is a democracy. The main distinction of a democratic form of government is the acknowledgement that the people are above the government, in that the government and its officials are beholden to the people. Accountability at the government level ensures that the citizens have the ability to exercise their power over the government. The most common expression of this citizen held power is the power to vote, thereby electing representatives to carry out the mandate of the people while removing those who fail that endeavor. The specific accountability measures are outlined in the Constitution, charters, and laws. It is also important to note that in the United States, government accountability applies at all levels of government and all branches and segments with the levels of government. Further, in addition to individual citizens, watchdog groups and the press help hold governments accountable. In recent times, there has been an increase of reporting from governments and their entities. These reports now form the basis for which determinations are made as to the effectiveness of that government or entity. These reports may be performance based and/or financial.

Governments owe their highest level of accountability to their citizens. This duty is recognized in that the citizens have the final word over government in the form of their voting power. It is important to note that different areas of government are accountable for different functions. It is important to identify the various functions of a specific government or government entity in order to properly and fairly hold them accountable. For example, the legislative branch of the national government is responsible for creating and budgeting for programs that meet the requirements and demands of citizens. However, it is the executive branch that is responsible for seeing that the programs created by the legislative branch are carried out in an effective and efficient manner. By understanding the various roles of government entities, citizens can better place praise and blame. Keep in mind that the media and other watchdog groups assist the public in maintaining government accountability.

Direct vs. indirect accountability

When discussing government accountability, there are two different types: (1) direct accountability and (2) indirect accountability. Direct accountability refers to the level of accountability held by those elected to office by the citizens themselves. This includes the chief executive and member of the legislature. However, this segment of government represents a relatively small number in light of the many lower level managers and employees that work for government entities. These other individuals are said to have indirect accountability to the citizens because they are not directly elected by the voting process. It is important to understand that direct versus indirect accountability is merely a descriptive term. It does not devalue the degree of accountability owed by the unelected people working within the government. In fact, as a whole it is the government managers and employees who have the greatest effect on government operations on a day-to-day basis.

Levels accountable to each other

Different levels of government can, and often due, hold each other accountable for their actions. The typical scenario is one viewed from the top down. That is to say, the national government oversees the states government and the state government oversees the local government. Perhaps the most common of these types of scenarios is where a program or project is created at the national level. This program or project is then passed on to the states who administer it locally. At each level, funds are provided so that the program or project can achieve its goals and objectives. A visible example of this is the funding of transportation projects. In many cases a project may originate at the national level with the United States Transportation Department. This entity then applies some of its funds to the state where the project is located. That state will, in turn, pass the funds to the locality where the work is undertaken. At each level, the "higher" government level oversees the activities of the "lower" government level to make sure that resources are properly utilized. In some cases, "lower" levels of government hold (or attempt to hold) "higher" levels of government accountable.

Branches accountable to each other

Government branches are accountable to each other. The United States' system of checks and balances and separation of powers assures that this is the case. For example, the executive branch proposes a budget every year (every two years in some states). However, the legislative branch may alter or amend the proposed budget in a myriad of ways. Likewise, the legislative branch may pass a law. However, this law must then go to the chief executive who can exercise his/her veto power. Subsequently, the chief executive's veto power may be overridden by obtaining the requisite votes in Congress. Additionally, both the executive and legislative branches are held accountable by the judiciary branch. For instance, the judiciary branch evaluates the constitutionality of laws passed by the legislative branch. If the law is deemed by the judicial branch to be unconstitutional the law is stricken. It is then up to the legislature to reform the law in a manner that is consistent with the constitution. Aside from checks and balances and separation of powers, government entities and their officials are often subject to accountability from other governmental components. For example, the Government Accountability Office oversees the handling of public funds by government entities.

Accountable to investors

Government officials are accountable to investors and creditors. The terms investor and creditor, in this context, refer to large groups of entities and people. The term investor takes on a different meaning when discussing government accountability than when discussing private sector entities. With the latter, investor usually refers to someone or some entity that owns equity in the private entity (these are referred to as publicly held). However, government entities do not issue stock. Therefore, their investors are different from those in the private sector. Government investors may include other governments and private entities that link with the United States government entity to complete a capital project. Government investors may also encompass government employees who invest their money in government retirement plans. Because of the finances at stake, government officials owe government investors a high level of accountability. The term government creditor refers to individuals and entities that purchase government bonds (or other debt instruments). It is imperative that the government remain accountable to government creditors in order to maintain a healthy market for government to access borrowed funds.

Government officials and managers are often held accountable by many different entities and individuals. Sometimes these sources even represent competing interests. For example, one government agency may oversee the timely progress of a particular project, while another may constantly monitor the outflow of funds applied to the project. To operate in this environment, a government manager can adopt one of three managerial positions: (1) reactive, (2) adaptive, or (3) strategic. A manager who is reactive tends to await the receipt of a mandate from his/her constituency before taking action. In this case the manager will not involve him/herself in the formation of the strategy or planning until such time as the governed group identifies its desires. An adaptive manager is a little more proactive in that he/she will attempt to anticipate the nature of the expected mandate and begin implementing strategies to best achieve the goals and objectives. Finally, the strategic manager takes a more aggressive role and involves him/herself with the actual decision making process of the community. This potentially gives the manager the opportunity to form mandates from the constituency.

Categories of accountability

Broadly speaking, government accountability originates in a particular government's constitution or charter. To provide greater detail as to what is expected from its government officials, each jurisdiction creates laws, ordinances, and regulations that further identify the specific things for which government officials will be held accountable. Generally, despite different nuances amongst different jurisdictions, there are four categories of accountability. The first category requires that money be collected and exhausted based on the provisions of a well planned budget. The second category seeks to make sure that operations are conducted such that they comply with all applicable laws, regulations, and policies. The third category of accountability strives to ensure that limited resources are utilized as efficiently as possible. The fourth category of accountability mandates that implemented programs realize there goals and objectives.

Federal Accounting Standards Advisory Board

The Federal Accounting Standards Advisory Board (FASAB) is a government entity charged with establishing accounting standards at the national level of government. In its own words, "The mission of the FASAB is to promulgate federal accounting standards after considering the financial and budgetary information needs of citizens, congressional oversight groups, executive agencies, and the needs of other users of federal financial information." FASAB establishes government accountability with respect to the following classifications: (1) funds are to be acquired and expended according to budgetary law, (2) fund are utilized to minimize waste and maximize program success, (3) operations encourage the vitality of the jurisdiction, and (4) governments establish policies that avoid waste of resources.

Governmental Accounting Standards Board

The Governmental Accounting Standards Board (GASB) is a government entity charged with establishing accounting standards at the state and local levels of government. As it states, "The mission of the Governmental Accounting Standards Board is to establish and improve standards of state and local governmental accounting and financial reporting that will result in useful information for users of financial reports and guide and educate the public, including issuers, auditors, and users of those financial reports."* Additionally, the GASB has identified five areas of government accountability: (1) acquiring and expending funds in accordance with budgetary law, (2) maximizing accountability through management functions, the configuration of the entity and internal controls, (3) proficiently attaining outputs, (4) reaching intended outcomes, and (5) instituting and updating entity policies.

Accountability between public and private entities

Accountability between public and private entities is similar in that both types of entities (and their management) are beholden to others on some level. For instance, private entities that are publicly held (stock is offered for sale to the public) have disclosure burdens that must be met. Primarily these requirements are imposed so that investors will have a fair opportunity to evaluate the financial strength of the company. Government accountability is a bit different in that its main focus is the efficient use of public funds. Unlike private entities, government entities operate solely on the money of its citizens (although this money may be collected in a number of different ways). As such, there is tremendous accountability requirements imposed on how government entities acquire and utilize these public funds. In the private sector, investors and regulators are only concerned with the legality and size of the profit. Furthermore, governments and government entities are often accountable to each other. In the private sector, individual entities work autonomously and are only subject to the relevant laws that govern their business.

Role in financial management

Merriam-Webster Online defines accountability as: "an obligation or willingness to accept responsibility or to account for one's actions." Financial accountability (and government accountability in general) is simpler in smaller governments. This is not to say that it is always *easier*, however. With smaller governments there are typically less officials, fewer constituents and more focused financial matters for review. Because our government operates on funds provided through the citizens (directly or indirectly), these citizens demand accountability as to how their money is being utilized. This is the specific role of financial management. Financial management focuses on how the public's limited resources are utilized to achieve the specific goals of the particular government entity being examined. Financial management accountability is typically judged based on various financial reports that are issued by the government entity which demonstrate their efficiency. Keep in mind that financial accountability doesn't just evaluate how the public funds are spent, but also how they are attained.

Private sector accountability

Private sector accountability has two primary objectives: (1) the private entity is to strive to be as profitable as possible (this is especially true in the case of publicly held private entities) and (2) to achieve this profitability in compliance with the laws of the jurisdictions in which it operates. Meanwhile, government accountability is far less clearly defined. Government entities are certainly expected to follow all of the relevant laws with regards to their operations and practices just like private entities, but it is the first objective listed above that creates the distinction. While private entities can point to a bottom line figure to demonstrate their efficiency and effectiveness, government entities often do not have that luxury. For example, most government entities spend more money than they generate. Therefore, profitability is a mute point. Further, it is often meaningless to compare government entities. For instance, one government entity may expend far less revenue than another similar entity. However, the former entity may also have undertaken and completed many civic projects that will greatly benefit its jurisdiction. Also, while both governments and private entities are concerned with perception, governments must pay particularly close attention. For example, a private entity can withstand some negative perception and still maintain profitability. On the other hand, negative publicity at the government level can lead to lost elections, phased-out government entities, and even impeachments.

Implementing accountability

As a starting point, governments and government entities must identify the items that are specific to their organization that require accountability. For example, a school district might highlight exam scores while a police department identifies arrests made as critical functions to their respective entities. Next the government entity should properly structure itself so that the specific functions carried out by the entity are done so in the best possible manner. Proper structuring can greatly assist accountability if it succeeds in pairing resources with those responsible for utilizing those resources to achieve specific results. This not only clearly identifies the role of employees within the organization, but allows management to easily identify in deficiencies within the organization. Government managers should also implement accountability studies. These studies should be undertaken periodically and are more inclusive than financial studies that generally only focus on compliance with generally accepted accounting principles. Accountability studies may evaluate how a program has been executed, the efficiency with which funds are being utilized, and to what extent the ultimate goal is being achieved.

Maintaining accountability

There are many groups and individuals that help maintain the accountability of government. For example, there are many watchdog groups whose sole mission is to hold government accountable. One such organization is the National Whistleblower Center. This organization advocates government accountability by vigorously defending government employees who step forward to report government misconduct. Similarly, the press holds a very prominent role and holding governments accountable. Through their various sources, members of the media can have a tremendous impact on government operations by uncovering misdeeds by government entities. Of course, the power of the media is limited by the level of concern of the observers of the discloser. That is to say, the media is more of a conduit of information to the citizens. At the forefront of government accountability are the actual individuals who work for the government. Both managers and employees have both the opportunity to perform their prescribed duties in an appropriate manner and to make it known when wrongdoing occurs within their government entity.

Government management cycle

As noted earlier, the government management cycle consists of the following stages:
1. planning
2. programming
3. budgeting
4. operations
5. accounting
6. reporting
7. auditing

Government accountability is critical at each stage of the management cycle. For example, during the planning cycle accountability is important because any missteps at this stage of the government management cycle could result in establishing goals for the government entity that are irrelevant or unattainable. Similarly, at the programming stage, accountability is important because this stage involves the determination of the most cost-effective methods of achieving the goals identified in the planning phase. Even the reporting phase requires accountability. This may seem strange since the purpose of reporting is to establish accountability. However, if the methods and procedures followed during the reporting phase are flawed, the information used by citizens to gauge overall accountability of the government entity may be misleading as to the effectiveness of the government entity and its management.

Legal foundations

Government accountability is not simply a concept that has permeated the political landscape of the United States. Without some legal foundation, the idea of government accountability would be unenforceable and hollow. The underlying source of government accountability is found at the national and state level in Constitutions. Additionally, local government charters also establish the groundwork for government accountability at their level. Specifically, in the preamble of the United States Constitution, the term "We the People" is identified as giving rise to government accountability on the national level of government. An example at the state level can be seen in the Constitution of the State of Tennessee. Specifically, Article one, Section one states: "That all power is inherent in the people, and all free governments are founded on their authority, and instituted for their peace, safety, and happiness; for the advancement of those ends they have at all times, an unalienable and indefeasible right to alter, reform, or abolish the government in such manner as they may think proper."

Various levels

As is the case with many broad concepts that are only mentioned at the constitutional or charter level, specific laws and regulations provide the details for government accountability. Additionally, the creation of government entities with a primary purpose of overseeing government operations demonstrates the presence of government accountability. For example, the Government Accountability Office was created in 1921 as a non-partisan audit, evaluation, and investigative arm of the legislative branch of the United States government. The primary focus of the Government Accountability Office is to oversee the collection and expenditure of public funds. In addition to specific government entities, there are many examples of specific statutory provisions at all levels of government that create government accountability. For example, South Carolina Code of Laws, Title 8, Chapter 13, Article 1 specifically addresses issues relating to campaign finance rules for public officers and employees. Additionally, there are countless reporting laws that require specific types of reports at specific times that contain specific information. These organizations and laws are present at all levels of government.

Stewardship

Merriam-Webster Online defines stewardship as "the careful and responsible management of something entrusted to one's care." The concept of stewardship summarizes the concept of government accountability to its citizens in the United States. While there are many reporting requirements and other accountability measures that take great care to safeguard the public interests with regards to government operations over specific and finite periods of time, it is important to understand that the responsibility of the government to act as a steward for its citizens is a more long-term endeavor. Stewardship refers to the government's duty to care for the security of its citizens well into the future. Intrinsic in this concept is the idea that assets and resources are precious and must be guarded for the well being of current and future generations.

Oversight hearing

The United States government is subject to the doctrines of separation of powers and checks and balances. In the context of government accountability, this means that various branches of government are subject to scrutiny by other branches. One example of this is oversight hearings. Oversight hearings are a tool used by the legislative branch of government to hold the executive branch accountable for its actions. Recall that the legislature creates programs, while the executive branch carries out these programs. Oversight hearings allow the legislative branch to analyze the effectiveness of the executive branch in carrying out its programs. Furthermore, the courts often intervene in oversight hearings to pass judgment on the effectiveness of the executive branch's activities.

Program evaluations

Program evaluations are a tool used by government managers and other officials. Program evaluations are conducted to gauge accountability for a specific government entity or operation. These studies can evaluate the accountability of the studied subject on several different levels. For example, a program evaluation may be conducted to determine if expenditures within the program are appropriate for the results that they are producing. On a broader scale, program evaluations can examine the program as a whole and determine its effectiveness. Furthermore, an essential component of program evaluations is relevance. Programs should always be tested not only for how competently they are operating, but whether or not the program itself is still relevant to meet the needs of the citizens.

Reports

Reports are a method by which government entities both assess and demonstrate accountability. At their most basic, reports compare and contrast what was intended to happen with what actually did happen. Reporting has become so prolific that it has its own stage of the government management cycle. Not surprisingly, the reporting stage of the government management cycle follows the operations and accounting stages. Government reports can be broken down into two categories: (1) financial and (2) performance. Constitutions and laws dictate that government entities compose various financial reports to reflect the flows of money throughout the organization. These financial reports must be generated in compliance with Generally Accepted Accounting Principles (GAAP). Performance reports are less regulated than financial reports. Performance reports use more than just financial data in an attempt to determine the effectiveness of a government entity at achieving its goals and objectives. Both financial and performance reports are created internally, and subject to external audits.

External audits

External audits are a critical component of government entity accountability. Government audits can be performed by a number of different groups. Internal audits are frequently conducted by government entities on themselves to gauge efficiency and compliance. However, it is external audits that carry the greatest weight from the public accountability perspective. Most of the time, the results of these external audits are made public. Once the government entity is apprised of the audit results, the entity should take appropriate action to address the negative findings and perpetuate the positive outcomes. The Government Accountability

Office is a United States Congressional entity that conducts many investigations, which support government accountability. The Government Accountability Office has developed standards to be employed when auditing government entities. These standards help make sure that audits are conducted by qualified auditors in such a way that the results reached will supply the greatest amount of accountability.

Media

A key distinguishing factor between the United States and other nations is the free press. The media, as the press is also referred to, is given very wide latitude in reporting almost anything it desires. A desired result of this media freedom is increased government scrutiny. One way in which the media plays a role in government accountability is through the evaluation and research of reports and data. Government entities often report large amounts of data that can be overwhelming for individual citizens to process and evaluate. Without some way to distill reporting data into something manageable for citizens, the results of government reporting requirements could prove fruitless. The government itself has taken some measures to ensure that its reporting results are more user friendly. However, the media has long played an important role in wading through voluminous, and often confusing, data to create an understandable description of a government entity's activities.

Ethics in Government

The term ethics is defined as "the discipline dealing with what is good and bad and with moral duty and obligation." The concept of ethics manifests itself in many ways. For example, ethics are at the root of many laws and regulations meant to check behavior. Less formally, societies generally form their own codes of conduct based on what they determine to be ethical behavior. However, as is the case with all formal rules for behavior, no authority can be everywhere at all times to monitor people's actions. As a result, the most important governor of one's conduct is the individual him/herself. Ethics within the context of government financial managers is no different. Because government financial managers are entrusted with controlling public funds, they must adhere to the highest of ethical standards. Additionally, they must be vigilant in evaluating the actions of those around them to ensure that public resources are not misused.

Certified Government Financial Managers

Certified Government Financial Managers must take great care to make sure that there actions appear and, in fact, are ethical. This emphasis of ethics is due to the fact that government financial managers hold positions of high public trust. Specifically, government financial managers deal directly with the oversight of public funds. Therefore, it is logical that government financial managers are governed by specific formal ethical guidelines. These guidelines were developed by the Association of Government Accountants (AGA). The AGA states that the objective of government financial managers is to achieve the highest level of professionalism so as to protect the public's interests. The AGA ethics code requires four needs be met in order for this objective to be met. These four needs are: (1) credibility, (2) professionalism, (3) quality of services, and (4) confidence. Additionally, the AGA spells out principles that are required of government financial managers in order to achieve the desired objectives.

These principles are:
- integrity
- objectivity
- competence and due care
- confidentiality
- professional behavior
- technical standards

Every profession demands some degree of ethics. Both the private and public sectors require ethical behavior of their employees and managers. Without some foundational ethical standards, businesses and organizations would be completely incapable of carrying out their intended purposes. This is especially true in the government environment. Particularly, government financial managers must employ the highest ethical standards. This is due mainly to the fact that government financial managers are central players in determining how public funds are handled by various government entities. The ethical duty of government financial managers not only covers their own actions, but extends to the actions of others. If a government financial manager becomes aware of unethical behavior, whatever necessary steps to stop such behavior should be taken. Furthermore, even the appearance of impropriety should be avoided. Government financial managers should take caution to avoid any conflicts of interests that could (or that could appear to) cloud their judgment with regard to government entity operations.

It should be clear that acting in a capacity for which one is improperly qualified would be unethical. Government financial managers are held to no less of a standard. Because government entities operate on public funds, the public should, and does, require that the financial managers of such entities are fully qualified to efficiently safeguard the public's funds. Specifically, this means that government financial managers should possess the requisite educational and practical background to perform the tasks required of their profession. This includes any specialized practical knowledge required by their specific position. Additionally, government financial managers should follow any guidelines that exist within their government entity or their profession (e.g., professional standards). Furthermore, government financial managers have a duty to oversee and guide underlings to someday become competent managers themselves. Finally, government financial managers demonstrate competency by only accepting projects that further the goals and objectives of their government entity and that can be properly completed within all relevant guidelines.

The Association of Government Accountants (AGA) has detailed specific objectives and principles regarding the ethical standards for government financial managers. These standards specifically apply to AGA members, but should also guide the actions of non-members as well. In addition to the guidelines established by the AGA, there are many sources of ethical standards that government finance managers should, and sometimes must adhere to. For example, many standard setting organizations exist at all levels of government. For obvious reasons, government finance manager ethics is just as important at the state and local levels of government as it is at the national level. Additionally, there are many governing bodies and accrediting organizations that are delineated by geography, profession, and other criteria that spell out their own criteria for ethical behavior that must be followed in order to maintain membership.

There are many cases of government employees and officials coming forward to report inefficient and unethical behavior that they observe in government entities. The offending behavior can range from misappropriated funds to misdeeds that actually put lives in danger. In 2005, Dr. Jonathan Fishbein claimed that officials at the National Institutes of Health disregarded health risks posed by the AIDS drug nevirapine. The purpose of the drug was to prevent the occurrence of AIDS in newborn babies in Africa. Dr. Fishbein's complaint did not condemn the drug's effectiveness, but rather the practices of those involved in the study. Dr. Fishbein claimed that the study was administered in such a poor manner that any results from the study could not be trusted and could lead to unnecessary deaths. Dr. Fishbein was fired as a result of his public disclosures, but he has sought protection under whistleblower laws.

Public interest

The word "public" is defined as "of, relating to, or affecting all the people or the whole area of a nation or state." This definition highlights that large group that is identified by using the term public. The interests of the public are obviously those concerns shared amongst those members of the group. Stated differently, public interest refers to the matters that are important to the well-being of citizens within a particular jurisdiction. This deference for the public interest is a unique role of government and differs greatly from private sector entities. Private sector entities serve the interests of their owners and, to a lesser extent, their employees. Private entities are only concerned with the public's welfare to the extent laws require or profitability is affected. Because serving the public interest means looking out for the welfare of a large group of diverse citizens, what constitutes promoting the public interest can change as the needs of the citizens change. Government finance managers play a critical role in making sure that government entities serve the public interest.

Acts of omission

In order for a government or government entities to serve the public interest, its employees and officials must serve the public interest. Serving the public interest can be achieved through acts of commission and acts of omission. To adequately protect the public interest, one omission that government employees and officials must make is the utilization of their situation for personal gain. Examples of attaining inappropriate benefits can be obvious and obscure. For example, a blatant misuse of government position is the receipt of cash for directing the award of a government contract. Additionally, although far less obvious, it is inappropriate for government employees and officials to receive even small gifts or tokens from civilians who deal with the government in their professional endeavors. Furthermore, this notion of disallowed personal benefit even extends to those that are tangentially associated with government employees and officials. This includes family members, social acquaintances, and personal business associates. Even the perception of exploiting government employment for personal gain undermines the public confidence and should be guarded against. This concept highlights that idea that working for the government, at any level, is truly public service.

Conflict of interest

Evaluate the following situation to determine if a conflict of interest exists.
<u>Situation</u>: Barbara is an employee at the State A Department of Transportation. Barbara is a finance manager for the Department of Transportation and in this capacity she is heavily involved with the funding of projects undertaken by the government entity. In particular, the State A Department of Transportation is accepting bids from outside contractors on a major street improvement project. One of the bidders is Barbara's brother-in-law. Barbara has not spoken to her brother-in-law for seven years as a result of a falling out between Barbara and her sister. Additionally, Barbara does not have direct authority over the bidding process. Barbara does, however, work closely with those people who do award the contracts. Answer: The fact that Barbara and her sister no longer communicate and, therefore, Barbara has no contact with her brother-in-law is of little significance. The fact remains that Barbara is related to someone seeking a benefit from the government entity she works for. The fact that Barbara does not have direct authority over the bidding process is persuasive. However, this fact is probably overcome by the fact that Barbara works closely with those that determine the contract bidding winners. Additionally, the fact that Barbara is a financial manager who oversees project funding adds complication to this situation. Finally, regardless of whether or not there is an actual conflict of interest, this situation gives rise to the appearance of a conflict. As such, this and similar situations should be avoided.

Conflicts of interest can have a negative effect of government entities in two ways. First, conflicts can cause government officials and employees to act in such a way that is not serving the public interest. Second, even if the conflict does not create any disservice to the public interest, the perception of the conflict can damage the public trust. Because of these negative aspects, the best method of dealing with a conflict is avoidance. However, barring preempting the conflict altogether, there are several options for mitigating the effects of conflicts of interest. For example, if the conflict arises as a result of one or a limited few within a government entity, those parties could remove themselves from the specific situation giving rise to the conflict. Additionally, the government entity could surrender their rights to the property that causes the conflict. This may not always be a viable option because preservation of resources is critical to government entities. Next, offending assets can be placed into a trust that acts as an independent middleman, thereby eliminating the offending relationship. Finally, the assets creating or resulting from a conflict can be sold.

Role of jointly governed organizations

A jointly governed organization is one that is created by representatives from multiple county or local governments. Once they are set up, the governments do not maintain an ongoing financial interest and are not responsible for the oversight of the organization. Rather, the organization has a board of directors that create by-laws, programs, and budgets. Cooperating school districts are a common jointly governed organization. They are founded to take advantage of regional resources and strive to create continuous improvement in all school districts that are part of the co-op rather than seeing improvement only in those school districts that have a greater share of resources. For example, the Cooperating School District of Greater Kansas City is a co-op of 29 school districts throughout the greater Kansas City area.

Financial management responsibilities and skills

Employment duties

It is generally understood that the jobs of government employees can be difficult. Because of sometimes conflicting roles, government entities have difficulty operating in such a way that results in the most efficient achievement of goals and objectives. Furthermore, these goals and objectives are constantly changing. Therefore, the employees that work for these government entities may find their roles complex and somewhat confusing. Despite these encumbrances, government employees are expected to make a good faith effort at achieving their job duties. Note that this requirement isn't asking that government employees be perfect; this would be an unattainable goal for any employee. However, government employees are expected to identify the tasks that need to be accomplished, allocate ample time to complete those tasks, perform their tasks at the highest competency level possible, and avoid waste or misuse of government time. To monitor government employee performance, detailed performance appraisals are often utilized.

Integrity

It is important to remember that government entities and government itself are merely reflections of their employees. This includes the rank and file as well as elected officials. Therefore, because integrity is expected of the government and its entities, integrity is required of government employees. In fact, the integrity of a government entity is directly proportional to the integrity of its employees. Each government entity shares the common overriding goal of serving the public interest. Without government employee integrity, government cannot achieve its primary purpose of serving the public interest. To demonstrate integrity, government employees should always monitor their professional behavior. For example, if a government employee makes a commitment to complete a project by a certain time that commitment should be met. More generally, government employees should avoid things that are against the public interests (in reality or perceived). Additionally, government employees should always make clear when they are speaking for themselves and not representing the government.

Serving the public interest

Serving the public interest is an overriding goal of all government entities. This goal is the unifying factor amongst a large number of government entities with very diverse goals, programs, and employees. Because of the importance of serving the public interest, the relevance of government employee integrity is not limited to actions taken by those employees during working hours. For instance, government employees are expected to follow all laws. This is true even in the case of laws that do not directly relate to their work responsibilities. This is different from private entities, which typically only concern themselves with employee conduct outside the office to the extent it negatively impacts the entity's profitability. In addition to generally following laws, government employees are expected to strictly adhere to laws and regulations pertinent to their government entity. For example, employees are subject to regular tax audits and can suffer negative evaluations, suspensions, and firing if they are not in full compliance with all tax laws. Additionally, government employees should always make clear when they are speaking for themselves and not representing the government.

Compromise

Government entities often have a multitude of goals and objectives. In many cases, these goals and objectives overlap and even contradict each other. To continue the operations of the government entity, compromise is often required to meet these conflicting targets. Additionally, limited government resources also create the need for compromise in government entities. For example, government entities may be limited as to time, funding, or manpower. In order to achieve the greatest number of goals and objectives with these limited resources, government managers must make certain compromises. Despite these valuable uses for compromise, it is imperative that compromise does not come at the cost of integrity. Remember that compromise may lead to the achievement of some goals and objectives, but the overriding goal of serving the public interest is paramount.

Objectivity and independence

It is important to always remember that the highest goal of government is to serve the public interest. Objectivity is defined as "expressing or dealing with facts or conditions as perceived without distortion by personal feelings, prejudices, or interpretations." Objectivity is important because it allows government employees to focus on their primary goal of serving the public interest. Where objectivity is not present, by definition something other than the protecting the public trust is influencing the government employee. Independent is defined as "not subject to control by others, not requiring or relying on something else." Independence of government employees is important for reasons similar to those requiring objectivity. Government employees should take preventative steps to ensure that they remain free from the control of anyone or anything that is misaligned with the public interest.

It is important to remember that the importance of practicing objectivity and independence by a government employee comes from the supreme goal of serving the public interest. An initial threshold in adopting objectivity and independence is the avoidance of any conflicts of interest. Conflicts of interest are defined as "a situation in which someone in a position of trust...has competing professional or personal interests." As seen by this definition, conflicts of interests can create goals that are not in sync with the public interest. This can lead to a wide range of government employee misdeeds. Everything from misappropriating funds to utilizing government property for personal gain can emerge from conflicts of interest. Not only can severe problems arise from the presence of conflicts of interest, but even the façade of conflict can create troubles. Apparent conflicts of interest are different in that the problems that they create are typically from outside the government entity. For example, where there is no actual conflict, but the public perceives that one exists with one or more government employees, the public trust is compromised.

Support for elected officials

In many cases, elected officials represent the "face" of government, or at least their particular government entity. In this role, it is important that government officials project an image of competency and trustworthiness. Government employees are a critical part of this. Elected officials depend of government employees to do their jobs effectively so that the government functions efficiently and goals and objectives are met. Additionally, elected officials rely on accurate data reporting from government employees in order to determine the effectiveness and relevance of the various government programs within their jurisdiction. Often, it is these determinations by elected officials that the public uses to determine the effectiveness of the elected official. This determination can lead to re-election, recall, or impeachment as the case may be. The duty of employees to support elected officials is not unchecked. Employees should support elected officials insomuch as that support serves the public interest. However, support of elected officials should not be given in any way that undermines the public trust (e.g., falsifying data to make an elected official's program appear effective).

Outside employment

It is important to remember that the overriding goal for government employees is to serve the public interest. To adequately achieve this goal, any conflicts of interest that could potentially (or appear to) impair a government employee's independence should be avoided. Any employment undertaken by a government employee outside of his/her government duties raises questions about the existence of a conflict. This is especially true where the outside employment involves duties that are closely related to those duties of the employee in his/her capacity as a government employee. Additionally, regardless of the government employee's extracurricular duties, problems can arise where the employee's outside employer has dealings with the employee's government entity. Various government entities may vary how they determine the existence of a conflict with regards to outside employment. Therefore, the government employee should always seek the counsel of his/her manager before taking any outside employment.

Employment after government service

It is important to remember that the overriding goal of government employees is to serve the public interest. To adequately achieve this goal, any conflicts of interest that could potentially (or appear to) impair a government employee's independence should be avoided. In the typical scenario, conflicts arise out of situations that occur during the government employee's tenure as a government employee. However, sometimes the government employee's actions with respect to his subsequent employment can impair his/her impartiality. Obviously, neither the government as a whole, nor any government entities have much say about employment taken by former employees. However, conflicts can arise when the subsequent employment is sought while the employee is still with the government. The classic example of this is a government employee dealing with a private entity in his/her capacity as a government employee. During the course of their dealings, the private entity expresses an interest in hiring the government employee and related discussions ensue. This can greatly impair the government employee's ability to remain impartial.

Receiving gifts

It is important to remember that the overriding goal of government employees is to serve the public interest. To adequately achieve this goal, any conflicts of interest that could potentially (or appear to) impair a government employee's independence should be avoided. It is not uncommon for businesses (especially private entities) to give gifts to those with whom a professional relationship has been established or where one is desired. In the private sector, nothing is thought of this practice. However, an obvious conflict is created where a government employee or official accepts gifts from a private individual or entity. Different government entities have specific rules with regards to the receipt of gifts, but the safest rule is to avoid them altogether. Sometimes, the presence of a prior relationship between a government employee and the private entity acts as a mitigating factor, but extreme caution should be exercised. Additionally, gifts within government entities should be avoided to the extent they are received from subordinates. This could give the impression that favorable job treatment is for sale in that government entity.

Government financial managers

Level of competence
Government financial managers can play any number of professional roles within government entities. Typically, the common thread amongst these roles is that they are an important function within the entity and they are very intertwined with the public trust. Because of these factors, a high level of competency is required of government financial managers. It should be noted that even the highest level of competency will not ensure perfection or flawless operations at the entity level. However, government financial managers are expected to put forth a good faith effort in performing their tasks. Elements of this good faith effort include maintaining independence, appropriately supervising employees, acknowledging when a project or task may be better suited to someone else's skill set, and preserving government resources. Additionally, to maintain the proper level of competency, government financial managers are expected to engage in continuing

education and otherwise keep abreast of current developments in their field. Specifically, the Association of Government Accountants requires that eighty hours of continuing education be completed every two years in order to maintain the designation of Certified Government Financial Manager.

Role

Government financial managers play a very important role in their government entities. For example, government financial managers often are heavily involved in the operations of the government entity. Specifically, financial managers are paramount figures in the effort to preserve government resources while striving to achieve maximum goals and outputs. In addition, government financial managers must undertake general management duties. These duties may include dealing with employee issues (e.g., hiring, firing, and evaluating) and overseeing the completion of projects by lower level employees. Finally, government financial managers are required to see that higher level officials are updated on the happenings of the government entity. Many of the tasks of government financial managers are dictated by laws and regulations.

Chief Financial Officer Act of 1990

Every employee and official of the government has responsibilities. These responsibilities all relate to serving the public interest. Logically, the higher you go within a government entity, in terms of leadership, the greater the responsibility. This concept is evident at the Chief Financial Officer level. At the national level, government Chief Financial Officers are subject to the provisions of specific legislation known as the Chief Financial Officer Act of 1990 (the Act). The main purpose of the Act was to improve the financial management of the United States Government. To achieve this goal, the Act created Chief Financial Officer positions at twenty-three federal agencies (note that the Department of Homeland Security has subsequently become the twenty-fourth federal agency to have a Chief Financial Officer position appointed to it). The Act also centralized authority over financial management with the Office of Management and Budget (OMB) by creating a Deputy Director for Management within the OMB. This deputy acts as the national government's chief financial management official.

Chief Financial Officers

As the financial manager of a major national government agency, Chief Financial Officers have broad responsibilities. These responsibilities include:
- "developing and maintaining integrated accounting and financial management systems; directing, managing, and providing policy guidance and oversight of all agency financial management personnel, activities, and operations; approving and managing financial management systems design and enhancement projects;

- developing budgets for financial management operations and improvements; overseeing the recruitment, selection, and training of personnel to carry out agency financial management functions;
- implementing agency asset management systems, including systems for cash management, credit management, debt collection, and property and inventory management and control; and
- monitoring the financial execution of the agency budget in relation to actual expenditures."

National, state, and local levels

The duties carried out by Chief Financial Officers are of extreme importance. While the numbers may be larger and the jurisdiction more widespread, national level Chief Financial Officers are no more important than their counterparts at the state and local levels. Other than scope of duties, titles of government Chief Financial Officers differ at various levels. For example, at the state level Chief Financial Officers are often referred to a State Controllers. The Colorado State Controller "manages the financial affairs of the state by providing financial information, issuing fiscal policies, ensuring timely recording of the budget, and providing accounting consulting services to state agencies." The principles which guide the actions of Chief Financial Officers at the state and local level are very similar to those that guide national level officers. Formally, state level Chief Financial Officers are subject to rules of specific laws and regulations which dictate their actions. Similarly, Chief Financial Officers at the local level are recognized through laws at the state level. Specifics regarding the duties of local level Chief Financial Officers are outlined in specific localities' charters and ordinances.

Various roles

Chief Financial Officers carry the extremely important burden of overseeing the financial operations of their government entity. As part of this role, Chief Financial Officers are privy to information about their government entity that other officers may lack. There are circumstances where this information is critical to the performance of other important activities of the government entity. In these circumstances, Chief Financial Officers should assume a leadership role. An example of this is in reporting. Government entities must file many reports. Often, Chief Financial Officers possess information that is important to the creation of these reports. Chief Financial Officers should be forthcoming with this information and assist, if not guide, other government managers in utilizing the information to fulfill their obligations. It is important, however, that Chief Financial Officers do not lose sight of the fact that their role is inherently secondary to the role of the government entity. As such, Chief Financial Officers should provide any support necessary to assist their government entity in achieving its stated goals and objectives.

Team development

The development of effective teams within government entities has been considered critical to government operations (and private sector operations for that matter) for a long time. Generically speaking, teams afford government entities the ability to spread considerable workloads among a greater number of employees thereby increasing efficiency and effectiveness. Recent trends in team building reflect a greater disregard for formal dividing both within and without government entities. This trend has emerged in large part because government entities are constantly being asked to handle more complex tasks with less available resources. One example of this trend is the development of work teams. Often, these teams are organized to include members from different areas of a government entity or even different government entities. Depending on the situation, these teams may be formed in response to a particular project or undertaking. Once the project is completed, the team will likely disband.

Promoting teamwork
Teamwork is often held up as a positive thing. Government managers must identify if and how teamwork will further the purpose of their government entity. Then the government manager should take the necessary steps to foster the appropriate type and level of teamwork that maximizes effectiveness and efficiency. Conceptually, promoting teamwork can be a difficult undertaking. This is due primarily to the competing interests involved. On the one hand, all employees need and desire recognition. On the other hand, the very nature of a team is to sacrifice one's sense of self for the good of the whole. Therefore, managers should be careful to acknowledge the accomplishments of teams without identifying any one person. Managers cannot ignore the celebration of a team's victories or the individual members may become disillusioned. However, too much individual praise and the team can be torn apart by jealousy and resentment. As with many roles of management, a proper balance should be sought.

Group dynamics
Proper team building is critical to effectively and efficiently achieving the goals and objectives of the government entity. However, disregard of group dynamics can negate the benefits that teams offer. For example, one benefit of team building is that complex tasks can be broken up and undertaken by many individuals. This decreases the time needed to complete the task. However, if so many people are included in the team that communication is difficult and the task is broken down into components that are too small, the project could bog down. Therefore, government managers must evaluate the reason for forming the team and utilize the appropriate number of team members. Additionally, government managers should be careful to the treat the team as an entity and not a composite of individuals. For example, a government manager should address negative actions taken by the team, and not the actions of a specific team member. Furthermore, government managers should continue to manage the individuals within their group, but must do so without undermining the chain of command that exists within specific teams.

Managers must always evaluate the effectiveness of their groups and make whatever alterations are necessary to maintain and increase the effectiveness of the group.

Conflict

Government managers are, by definition, leaders of their government entities. The groups led by government managers are comprised of individuals. These individuals often come from different backgrounds and have different viewpoints. Because of this, government managers must inevitably deal with conflict within their groups. The conflict that arises within a government entity may come from personality conflicts or disagreements regarding work issues. The nature of the conflict influences how a manager should deal with the conflict. For example, personality based conflicts require empathy on the part of the dissenters. Hopefully, through viewing things from each other's perspective, the disagreeing parties can reach a workable understanding. It is the government manager's job to facilitate this process. Professional, as opposed to personal, differences may be easier or harder to resolve depending on how impassioned the parties are about the issue that is the subject of the dispute. The government manager should intervene and settle the matter at dispute only if the parties cannot settle it themselves in acceptable manner. If the government manager must involve him/herself to settle the issue, a workable middle ground should be sought. If it is necessary for the government manager to settle the dispute by favoring one party over the other, then the government manager should take care to validate the "losing" party.

Mediation and arbitration: Mediation is defined as "intervention between conflicting parties to promote reconciliation, settlement, or compromise." When a dispute amongst parties within a government entity becomes such that it is apparent that the parties will be unable to settle the matter solely between themselves, government managers may involve a mediator. Mediation may vary from mediator to mediator and from issue to issue as to the formality of the process utilized to achieve resolution. However, the general idea that the goal of mediation is to facilitate agreement amongst the parties is constant. To achieve the goal of dispute resolution, mediators will typically meet with each party separately to better understand their positions. Mediators then will usually bring the parties together to achieve some middle ground through mutual understanding. To be most effective, the mediator should try to minimize the emotional aspect of the dispute. The mediator should also emphasize the positives of the resolution for each party in order to help the parties reach their own resolution.

The definition of arbitration is "the hearing and determination of a case in controversy by an arbiter." Arbitration is a very similar process to mediation. The main difference, however, is that with arbitration the facilitator (arbitrator) compels the outcome that he/she believes to me most appropriate.

Environment

The nature of government work has changed dramatically over recent years. Public demands for increased provision of government services coupled with public demand for more economically efficient operations and greater accountability have greatly increased the requirements of government entities and their employees. These increased requirements have resulted in several different manifestations. For instance, to track efficiency, greater reporting is demanded of government entities. The requisite efficiency and accountability at the entity level also flows down to the government employees. Therefore, it is imperative that government managers monitor their environment so that these greater demands are met. Specifically, government managers must create an environment that emphasizes productivity, inspires employees, provides employee growth, and allocating work equally.

Increasing productivity

The public demands ever increasing productivity and efficiency on the part of government. This places tremendous strain on government entities to increase their outputs while limiting their resource expenditures. To achieve this, government managers must be much attuned to maximizing the productivity of their government entity. At first blush it may seem logical for a government manager to evaluate the employees of government entity and look for any "weak links" in the organization. However, the more advisable approach is to examine "how" the government entity operates rather than "who" operates the government entity. This is because even highly skilled and dutiful workers can yield poor results if the design of the entity within which they work is flawed. Therefore, government managers must carefully evaluate the effectiveness of the entity set-up itself. For example, government employees should be very clear as to their chain of command. This includes the managers and any other employees that they must answer to, as well as a definitive understanding of who their customers are. Additionally, the organization of the government entity must be evaluated to ensure that the entity is still well suited to accomplish its changing goals and objectives, and remain compliant with all laws and regulations.

Motivating

It is critical that every government entity is staffed with motivated employees. Everything facet of a government entity could be perfect including its management and organization, and still inefficiencies would exist if the employees lack proper motivation. The topic of motivation is somewhat controversial in that it is hard to determine whether or not people can truly motivate other people. However, it is generally acknowledged that managers can take actions that will foster motivation. Perhaps the most difficult thing about motivation from a government manager's perspective is that their employees are often motivated by different things. Additionally, what motivates an employee currently may cease to motivate them in the future. Although difficult, it is important for government managers to tune into what effectively motivates their employees and constantly seek out better and more updated methods. Additionally, it is important for managers to understand that employees of different skill and ability levels can all be motivated. For example, even though an employee is a tremendous worker and always produces quality work products, his/her motivators should be identified so that their productivity can, at least, be maintained if not increased even further.

Developing employees

It is very important that managers continually develop their employees. The benefits that result from this development are many and vary depending on whose perspective is considered. From the employee's perspective, continual development can increase the employee's motivation for his/her job. Additionally, employees may derive a greater sense of fulfillment from their jobs as a result of increased development. This feeling often results when a manager or employing entity demonstrates confidence in the employee by providing them with additional training. Government managers also benefit from the development of their employees. For example, as a whole the more trained a manager's employees, the more capable they will be at accomplishing the goals and objectives of the entity. This increased training also acts to ensure that the competency levels of the employees are at an acceptable level. Additionally, it is important for government managers to keep their employees trained regarding the continuously changing technology landscape. Understanding new technology, while not part of the core duties of the entity, may help the employees better perform those core duties. Government managers should actively encourage the development of their employees. This should be done by supporting an employee's request for training and seeking training opportunities for employees.

Maintaining balanced workloads

A recent trend among government entities is a blurring of dividing lines. In other words, projects and assignments are more frequently drawing employees from different government entities in order to take advantage of specific skills and experiences to maximize effectiveness and efficiency. While this trend of cross-assignments is beneficial to government operations as a whole, it makes the task of balancing workloads within government entities difficult. Maintaining balanced workloads within government entities is important to preserve the effectiveness and efficiency of individual government entities. To properly balance workloads, government managers should take the varying capabilities of each of their employees into consideration. For example, some employees may be able to successfully manage several projects at once, while other may need to focus on one project at a time. This consideration of individual competencies may outline training needs that exist within the entity as well. In balancing the workload, government managers should include their employees in the process. This allows every employee in the entity to understand the full workload and understand their specific responsibilities. Additionally, government managers should include their employees in the process of establishing the criteria upon which the completion of a project will be judged. This helps to communicate what is expected of employees at the front end of a project.

Communicating effectively

Government entities are under constant pressure to take on expanding responsibilities, produce results faster, and do so with diminishing resources. These increased demands on government entities require effective communication. Communication within the government entity is important so that government employees are very clear as to the overall goals of the entity they are a part of. Additionally, internal communication is critical so that individual employees are clear as to what their duties are and what is expected of them. Government managers must also communicate with decision makers outside of their government entity. This is necessary so that those decision makers understand the goals and objectives being met by the entity. With this information, the decision makers can make appropriate judgments regarding the entity. Once information is communicated to government managers, it is important that the managers utilize the information in a manner that helps the entity best achieve its goals and objectives.

Flow of information

The exchange of information within a government entity is critical to ensure that the employees understand the overall goals of the entity as well as their specific duties. Information is also important inasmuch as it notifies government managers as to the effectiveness of the entity and areas where there could be improvement. Information typically flows from the top down. This means that government managers typically receive information first and their employees are dependant upon the managers to communicate the information. Managers should be very forthcoming with all information that is relevant to their employees. This would include any change in goals or operations of the government entity as well as any specific alterations to duties within the entity. Technology (e.g., email and software) can be utilized to increase information sharing within a government entity. However, government managers should identify when personal communication is more appropriate. For example, sensitive information that relates to an individual or small group of employees may be best communicated face-to-face. In addition to traditional channels, information can be obtained through personal networks. These networks consist of individuals who communicate as a result of a specific relationship. The networks can be formal, informal, professional, social, and even casual.

The flow of information, both within and without a government entity is critical to that entity's performance. However, despite the value of this information, the transfer of too much information can create a negative situation. For example, government employees can become confused as to their roles within their entity if they are bombarded with the duties and expectations of the entity as a whole. Additionally, government managers must determine how they want to receive information reporting from their employees. It may be tempting to request every detail, but managers should be judicious in the amount of information they receive from their employees. Having concise and succinct reports means that managers can process information efficiently and make necessary changes. Managers must also carefully screen the information that flows to their employees. The information conveyed should be relevant to those specific employees and should communicate their roles, duties, and expectations as to specific projects. Finally, government managers should also eliminate the disclosure of sensitive information.

Keeping informed

Information typically flows down. That is to say, government managers and other executives tend to receive information first and then relay that information down to their employees. However, the opposite is true of reporting information. This information tends to be made up of results of activities undertaken by the government entity. This information is first reported to the manager of the government entity so that the results of the entity's operations can be evaluated and shortcomings can be addressed. However, this information should not stop there. It is important for government managers to openly communicate their entity's results to their superiors and even to legislators. Obviously, the entity manager's superiors have a stake in the success or failure of the government entity. But keeping legislators informed as to the operations of a government entity can pay large dividends when it is time to pass budget laws. Government managers should be very accommodating of legislators in order to acquaint their entity with these important decision makers.

Federal government control of monetary policy

The Federal Reserve is ultimately responsible for monetary policy in the United States. The Federal Reserve is tasked with continuing to grow the US economy while keeping an eye on inflation. There is a healthy level of inflation that the Federal Reserve tries to maintain (depending on the economist, this usually can be anywhere between 2% and 3%). The Federal Reserve has multiple tools at its disposal, including controlling interest rates (via the discount rate) and money supply and overseeing banking regulations in general, including the amounts that a bank must keep in their reserves. Generally, the Federal Reserve tries to control the flow of money through discount rate changes; however, the Federal Reserve does have the ability to be what is called the "lender of last resort" in that it can print additional money to bail out an organization or an entire industry, as has occurred in the past.

Legal aspects of the government budget

The federal budget involves a five-step process—in essence, if any of these steps do not occur, the federal budget does not get passed, and as a result, the government and governmental agencies shut down because they do not have enough funds in their coffers to pay employees or maintain services. Below is an overview of each of the five steps:

1. The fiscal year for the United States runs from October 1 to September 30. The budgetary process begins with the president of the United States sending a proposed budget to Congress.
2. Congress reviews the proposal, and the House Committee on the Budget and the Senate Committee on the Budget each write their own budget resolutions—these resolutions include the spending limits for all of the federal agencies to ensure that they do not exceed their budgets. The two groups come to a consensus on the budget resolution, which is then voted on separately in the House of Representatives and the Senate.
3. Next, both the House Appropriations Committee and the Senate Appropriations Committee review the spending limits written into the budget resolution and write appropriations bills based on these amounts. These are sent to the House and Senate, respectively, for a vote.
4. The House and Senate debate the merits of the appropriations bills and iron out any items of concern. Then the appropriations bills are brought to a vote in both chambers.
5. Once passed in both chambers, the president signs each appropriations bill, and the budget is officially passed into law.

Executive branch control of spending

During the budget execution process, both the House of Representatives and the Senate form committees to help ensure that spending limits are assigned appropriately to federal agencies. The main way in which the executive branch controls spending is via appropriations bills, which are created by the appropriations committees. An appropriation bill lays out exactly how much money can be given to a federal program during the upcoming fiscal year. There are 12 appropriations subcommittees that are formed to discuss, debate, and ultimately create the 12 different appropriations bills that will be signed by the president. The appropriations subcommittees include the following:

1. Agriculture, Rural Development, and Food and Drug Administration (FDA)
2. Commerce, Justice, and Science
3. Defense
4. Energy and Water
5. Financial Services and General Government
6. Homeland Security
7. Interior and Environment
8. Labor, Health and Human Services, and Education
9. Legislative

10. Military Construction and Veterans Affairs
11. State and Foreign Operations
12. Transportation, Housing, and Urban Development

Practice Test

Practice Questions

1. Which system refers to the three levels of U.S. government working together on an equal basis to ensure that the fundamentals of the Constitution are followed?
   a. Allocation of services
   b. Checks and balances
   c. Separation of powers
   d. Functional consolidation

2. Which power is not granted to Congress under the Constitution?
   a. Regulating the value of money
   b. Declaring war
   c. Creating federal courts superior to the Supreme Court
   d. Levying and collecting taxes

3. The purpose of congressional oversight is to...
   a. review the actions of the executive branch
   b. review, monitor and supervise federal agencies and programs
   c. oversee the implementation of laws made by the judicial branch
   d. conduct congressional investigations into national matters

4. Which of the following is not a type of governmental entity?
   a. General purpose government
   b. Special purpose government
   c. Quasi-governmental entity
   d. Interim government

5. Which statement characterizes the concept of popular sovereignty?
   a. Citizens have ultimate authority over a government through the ballot
   b. The state legislature controls the actions of the state government
   c. A state's laws are independent of federal laws
   d. The individual is the controller of the individual's life

6. How are spending levels in congressional budget resolutions measured?
   a. Federal revenues
   b. Budget authority and outlays
   c. Offsetting collections and offsetting receipts
   d. The budget deficit and the federal debt

7. How is earmarking different from the appropriations process?
    a. Earmarking directs an amount of money toward a federal agency
    b. Earmarking directs an undetermined amount of money toward a federal project
    c. Earmarking directs a specific amount of money toward a particular project
    d. Earmarking and the appropriations process are the same

8. Which statement concerning the tax expenditure budget is accurate?
    a. The budget reduces the income tax liabilities of individuals and businesses
    b. The budget indicates where income tax revenues are spent
    c. The budget increases the income tax liabilities of individuals and businesses
    d. None of the above

9. Intergovernmental grants are considered beneficial to local governments when...
    a. local governments have a surplus of tax revenue
    b. local governments require short term funding
    c. local governments participate in solving problems that affect the national well being
    d. local governments require funding and guidance to find solutions to public problems

10. The government would implement a user fee for all purposes except...
    a. increasing costs
    b. budget restrictions
    c. decreasing demands
    d. to provide special services

11. Bond covenants requiring or forbidding certain actions of the issuer are specified...
    a. in the bond indenture
    b. in the bond underwriting agreement
    c. on the bond issuer's website
    d. in the prospectus

12. What is the purpose of the Chief Financial Officers Act of 1990?
    a. Effective general and financial management of the Federal government
    b. Improve accounting systems, financial management and internal control of the Federal government
    c. Provide complete, reliable, timely, and consistent financial information regarding the Federal government
    d. All of the above

13. Which federal government agency was given greater financial management authority by the Chief Financial Officers Act of 1990?
    a. The Council of Economic Advisers
    b. The Office of Management and Budget
    c. The Secretary of Commerce
    d. The Secretary of the Treasury

14. Which is one of the responsibilities of the Office of Federal Financial Management?
    a. Establishing government financial management policies
    b. Providing performance measurement and performance audits
    c. Providing financial reporting to the executive branch
    d. Providing financial reporting to the legislative branch

15. What set of standards is used when performing financial and performance audits of government agencies?
    a. AICPA audit standards
    b. Institute of Internal Auditors
    c. GAGAS
    d. INTOSAI Auditing Standards

16. The purpose of oversight hearings is to...
    a. review the annual financial audit of a federal agency
    b. focus on the quality of federal programs
    c. focus on the performance of government officials
    d. both B and C

17. The Code of Ethics of the Association of Governments Accountants obligates its members to be accountable for all conduct except...
    a. compliance with the standards and rules of the position of financial manager
    b. personal responsibility for actions and inactions
    c. reporting others that do not comply with the Code of Ethics
    d. consideration for the long-term interest of the government and its citizens

18. Which scenario depicts a financial manager not acting in the public interest?
    a. Implementing systems and procedures so that information technology can be used to manage government programs
    b. Relying on outside information to make recommendations regarding the feasibility of a program
    c. Making a determination of the effectiveness of an internal control system
    d. Formulating plans to use financial resources to address public policy issues

19. Which circumstance would prompt an investigation of a government financial manager for possibly violating the Code of Ethics of the Association of Government Accountants (AGA)?
    a. A financial manager has been subpoenaed by a court of law
    b. The AGA receives a complaint against a financial manager
    c. A financial manager has been charged with a criminal offense
    d. A financial manager makes an inaccurate statement regarding a government agency's financial statements

20. Which of the following is not a disciplinary action that may be taken against a financial manager that violated the Association of Government Accountants' Code of Ethics?
    a. Verbal warning
    b. Fines and monetary penalties
    c. Suspension of membership
    d. Payment of the costs of the investigation

21. How is "best practices" defined when referring to an Enterprise Resource Planning system?
    a. The system is free of viruses
    b. The system uses methods that are needed by all users and cannot be changed
    c. The system is modular and automated
    d. The software reflects the most effective way to perform each business process

22. Which component of a comprehensive fraud program is used to detect fraud patterns and identify future fraud risks?
    a. Data effectiveness
    b. Audit and investigation effectiveness
    c. Program effectiveness
    d. None of the above

23. Which is not a category of performance measures?
    a. Input measures
    b. Process measures
    c. Outcome measures
    d. Data measures

24. The purpose of information technology application controls is to...
    a. ensure the applications do not contain any viruses
    b. ensure transactions are processed accurately and completely
    c. reduce the duplication of data
    d. help predict areas where fraud may occur

25. The purpose of a performance management system is to...
   a. predict areas where employees are not complying with job descriptions
   b. improve employee confidence
   c. ensure the goals and objectives of the government agency are achieved
   d. ensure employees are effectively managed

Answers and Explanations

1. B: Checks and balances. The checks and balances system allows the executive, judicial and legislative branches of government to work together to maintain the fundamentals of the Constitution. The legislative branch makes laws, can override presidential vetoes, and sets jurisdiction of the court. The executive branch executes the laws, appoints judges, and can call emergency sessions of Congress. The judicial branch interprets laws, and investigates whether actions of the legislative and executives branches comply with the Constitution. This separation of powers helps to ensure transparency and prevents one branch of government from dominating the other two in that each branch checks on the actions performed by the other branches.

2. C: Creating federal courts superior to the Supreme Court. Article I, Section 8 of the Constitution grants Congress the power to create tribunals inferior to the Supreme Court, as well as the following powers:
- Lay and collect taxes, duties, imposts and excises
- Provide for the common defense and general welfare of the United States
- Borrow money on the credit of the United States
- Regulate commerce with foreign nations, and among the several states, and with the Indian tribes
- Coin money, regulate the value thereof, and of foreign coin, and provide for the punishment of counterfeiting
- Establish post offices and post roads
- Promote the progress of science and useful arts
- Declare war, raise and support armies, provide and maintain a navy, and make rules for the government and regulation of the land and naval forces

3. B: Review, monitor and supervise federal agencies and programs. Congressional oversight is the review, monitoring, and supervision of federal agencies and programs. Congress exercises this power through the congressional committee system. Congress does not have the authority, however, to investigate the actions of the executive branch; it cannot review executive branch records nor issue subpoenas for documents or testimony from the executive branch. Congressional oversight provides for:
- efficient, economic, and effective governmental operations
- the evaluation of programs and performance
- the detection and prevention of poor administration, waste, and abuse
- the protection of civil liberties and constitutional rights
- an assurance that executive policies reflect the public interest

4. D: Interim government. General purpose governments are local governments such as county, municipal or township governments that operate in accordance with state laws and constitutions. These governments perform functions which may include public works, public safety, recreation, public health objectives and law

enforcement. Special purpose governments are independent government entities that operate separately from general purpose local governments. Special purpose governments provide specific services such as hospitals, fire protection, water, sewer and environmental monitoring. Quasi-governmental entities are legal entities created and supported by a government, but managed privately, to perform commercial activities on behalf of the government.

5. A: Citizens have ultimate authority over a government through the ballot. Popular sovereignty, or sovereignty of the people, asserts that the legitimacy of a state is determined by the consent of the people. Voters control the actions of the state through the ballot process. Residents of a state make decisions by voting on issues, political candidates, referendums, and laws.

6. B: Budget authority and outlays. Spending levels in congressional budget resolutions are measured in dollars, and are based on budget authority and outlays. Budget authority, granted by law, allows an obligation that will result in the outlay of federal funds. Budget authority is classified by the period of availability, the timing of congressional actions, or by determining the available amount for the outlay. The outlay is the actual disbursement by the Treasury; the payment made to liquidate an obligation. Outlays during a fiscal year may be for obligations incurred in a prior year, or for those in the current year.

7. C: Earmarking directs a specific amount of money toward a particular project. Earmarking is a provision made by the legislative branch of government that specifies that a specific dollar amount is to be spent on a specific project. In addition, an earmark may direct specific exemptions from taxes or mandated fees. Earmarks can be classified as either Hard (hardmarks) or Soft (softmarks). Hardmarks are allocated through legislation so they have the effect of law, and are binding. Softmarks are found in the text of Congressional Committee reports and do not have the effect of law, but are treated as binding.

8. A: The budget reduces the income tax liabilities of individuals and businesses. The tax expenditure budget consists of the estimated revenue losses to the federal government due to exclusions, exemptions, deductions, credits, deferrals, and preferential rates in the tax code. These tax reductions reduce the income tax liabilities of individuals and businesses. The tax expenditure budget is estimated by the Office of Tax Analysis of the Treasury Department, and the Congressional Joint Committee on Taxation. This information is then published by the Office of Management and Budget.

9. D: Local governments require funding and guidance to find solutions to public problems, Intergovernmental grants flow from the federal government to local governments to help solve problems. Local governments often look to the federal government for funding and guidance so help solve a public problem. In these cases, the federal government is better able to raise revenue and the local governments are able to use the revenue to implement policies. Intergovernmental grants may be

used to build new roads, increase police services, and provide for educational excellence. There may be restrictions on these intergovernmental grants.

10. C: Decreasing demands. Governments charge user fees for a variety of reasons. Among them are: to recover the costs of operating a facility, to avoid abuse and inappropriate behavior, to decrease or regulate demand, and to record the number of users. The decision to charge a user fee must be considered on an individual project basis. Different facilities and programs may have different perceptions with the public that uses the facilities. The public may easily pay a fee for some services but have reservations about paying a fee for another service. User fees may be necessary when the cost of a service increases, there are budget restrictions, a need to charge for a special service, demand for the service increases, or to control the behavior of the users.

11. A: In the bond indenture. The bond indenture is a contract that specifies the terms of the bond, the coupon rate, the period to maturity, and special features of the bond. The indenture is summarized in the bond prospectus. The indenture contains a bond covenant, an agreement between the bond's issuer and holder that can either require or forbid specified actions. A positive bond covenant requires the issuer to perform certain actions. A negative bond covenant forbids the issuer from performing specific actions.

12. D: All of the above. The purpose of the Chief Financial Officers Act of 1990 includes:
- Effective general and financial management practices of the federal government by establishing a Deputy Director for Management in the Office of Management and Budget, establishing an Office of Federal Financial Management headed by a Controller, and designating a Chief Financial Officer in each executive department and in each major executive agency in the federal government
- Improvement in accounting systems, financial management, and internal controls in each agency of the Federal Government, assuring reliable financial information and the deterrence of fraud, waste, and abuse of government resources
- Producing complete, reliable, timely, and consistent financial information for use by the executive branch of the government and the Congress in the financing, management, and evaluation of Federal programs

13. B: The Office of Management and Budget. The Chief Financial Officers Act of 1990 was established to improve the financial management of the federal government. The Act also set standards for financial performance and financial disclosure, and requires each federal agency to employ a Chief Financial Officer. The Office of Management and Budget is charged with overseeing these Chief Financial Officers through the Deputy Director for Management, which is the chief financial management official for the federal government.

14. A: Establishing government financial management policies. The Office of Federal Financial Management is a part of the Office of Management and Budget. The Office of Federal Financial Management is responsible for the financial management policy of the federal government. Responsibilities include implementing the financial management improvement priorities of the president, establishing financial management policies of executive agencies, and carrying out the financial management functions of the Chief Financial Officers Act. The Office of Federal Financial Management ensures that the government spends taxpayers' money responsibly, and that financial information is communicated accurately and effectively so that informed decisions are made about the management of government programs and policy implementation.

15. C: GAGAS. Generally Accepted Government Auditing Standards (GAGAS), or the Yellow Book, are the rules and processes for the financial and performance audits of government agencies, established by the U.S. Government Accountability Office. The GAGAS standards include independence, due care, continuing professional education, supervision, and quality control. The GAGAS standards are used for federal government audits, local government performance audits, and local government financial audits performed by Certified Public Accountants. Performance audits evaluate the performance of a government program or project compared to the objectives of the project or program. The AICPA (American Institute of Certified Public Accountants), Institute of Internal Auditors, and INTOSAI are autonomous, non-governmental professional organizations.

16. D: Both B and C. Oversight hearings are used to review the quality of federal programs and the performance of government officials. The goal of an oversight hearing is to improve the efficiency, economy, and effectiveness of government operations. In addition, oversight by governing authorities is used to detect poor administration, waste and abuse, and illegal and unconstitutional conduct. As a result of this process, the general public becomes informed of the activities of federal programs and government officials, giving the public an opportunity to evaluate executive policies to keep them in the public interest.

17. C: Reporting others that do not comply with the Code of Ethics. The Association of Government Accountants encourages its members to serve in the public interest with the highest ethical principles. Through its Code of Ethics, financial managers are provided with standards of behavior and guidance for making ethical decisions. In order to foster a sense of accountability, members have the obligation to:
- Become familiar with, and abide by, the expectations, standards and rules of the position and to seek out information needed to interpret and apply them
- Accept personal responsibility for the consequences of actions and inactions
- Take into account the long-term interest of the government and its citizens

18. B: Relying on outside information to make recommendations regarding the feasibility of a program. In addition to providing sound accounting, accurate reporting, and effective financial management, a government financial manager is responsible to the public. Acting in the public interest, the financial manager is first and foremost concerned with the collective well-being of the community of people and institutions he serves. The public depends on the financial manager to be objective and to have integrity, contributing to the confidence on the part of the public that government is functioning in an orderly fashion.

19. B: The AGA receives a complaint against a financial manager. There are two reasons why the Association of Government Accountants (AGA) would investigate a financial manager for a violation of the Code of Ethics: when complaints are received from members and non-members and when the AGA receives information from other sources. The Ethics Committee is authorized to investigate allegations or inquiries, determine the validity of the allegations and issue disciplinary action to members and CFGMs. The AGA Ethics handbook describes the investigatory process in detail.

20. B: Fines and monetary penalties. Within the Association of Government Accountants, the Hearing Panel advises the Professional Ethics Board of its decision on the charges levied against the accused financial manager and on the disciplinary actions to be imposed. The Hearing Panel also submits a written report to the Professional Ethics Board containing the results of the hearing, an explanation of the issues, evidence and testimony, and the recommendation. Disciplinary actions may include:
- Remedial action such as additional education for the member or CGFM
- A verbal warning
- Censure, including a written reprimand to membership file and CGFM Board
- Suspension of membership for a specified period of time
- Termination of membership and/or CGFM Certificate
- Payment of the costs of investigation

21. D: The software reflects the most effective way to perform each business process. A best practice is an activity found successful in accomplishing a task, often determined by qualitative comparisons between the activities of similar entities. In Enterprise Resource Planning (ERP) systems, best practices include the software enabling the most effective way to perform each business process. This often entails customizing the system configuration, documentation, system testing, and end user training to the ERP system's end user's specific needs. ERP vendors realize their "off the shelf" products may need modification to enable those needs to be met. Following best practices helps to simplify compliance with industry regulations.

22. B: Audit and investigation effectiveness. There are three components of a comprehensive fraud program:

- Data effectiveness allows decisions to be made more efficiently and with less risk. It also enables government to standardize data to more easily identify duplicate information
- Audit and investigation effectiveness enables the detection of fraud patterns so that future risks can be identified and predicted. Detecting these schemes and patterns helps prevent fraud
- Program effectiveness monitors activities and threats to help prevent instances of fraud. It also identifies areas within the organization that can be improved so that best practices can be implemented

23. D: Data measures. There are four categories of performance measures:

- Input measures determine the resources used. Types of inputs that are measured include financial data, number of transactions processed, labor hours and equipment time used
- Process measures evaluate the number of inputs used to create outputs. These measures determine efficiency, such as productivity rates and cost figures
- Output measures quantify deliverables. Examples of output measures include the number of products sold or customers serviced.
- Outcome measures determine the results of the products or services delivered by comparing the actual activity to the planned activity. Examples include percentage of defective products or customers satisfied with services received

24. B: Ensure that transactions are processed accurately and completely. Information technology application controls are specific to a particular routine, operation, or software system. Application controls are used for transaction processing such as accounts payable, payroll, and inventory tracking. The purpose of application controls is to ensure that transactions are processed accurately and completely. These controls also ensure that each transaction has the proper authorization before being processed. In addition, application controls ensure that processing errors are prevented, detected, and corrected when they occur. While general controls apply to the entire computer operations, application controls must be reviewed individually for each application.

25. C: Ensure that the goals and objectives of the government agency are achieved. Performance management is a system of performance standards against which actual performance is reported, monitored, and compared. It helps to ensure that pre-determined goals are communicated, and that action is taken to achieve those goals. When actual performance differs from desired performance, an effective performance management system determines the cause of the difference, takes corrective action, and would possibly adjust goals, if needed. An effective

performance management system in a government setting can be an important component to improve public management and increase public confidence.

Secret Key #1 - Time is Your Greatest Enemy

Pace Yourself

Wear a watch. At the beginning of the test, check the time (or start a chronometer on your watch to count the minutes), and check the time after every few questions to make sure you are "on schedule."

If you are forced to speed up, do it efficiently. Usually one or more answer choices can be eliminated without too much difficulty. Above all, don't panic. Don't speed up and just begin guessing at random choices. By pacing yourself, and continually monitoring your progress against your watch, you will always know exactly how far ahead or behind you are with your available time. If you find that you are one minute behind on the test, don't skip one question without spending any time on it, just to catch back up. Take 15 fewer seconds on the next four questions, and after four questions you'll have caught back up. Once you catch back up, you can continue working each problem at your normal pace.

Furthermore, don't dwell on the problems that you were rushed on. If a problem was taking up too much time and you made a hurried guess, it must be difficult. The difficult questions are the ones you are most likely to miss anyway, so it isn't a big loss. It is better to end with more time than you need than to run out of time.

Lastly, sometimes it is beneficial to slow down if you are constantly getting ahead of time. You are always more likely to catch a careless mistake by working more slowly than quickly, and among very high-scoring test takers (those who are likely to have lots of time left over), careless errors affect the score more than mastery of material.

Secret Key #2 - Guessing is not Guesswork

You probably know that guessing is a good idea. Unlike other standardized tests, there is no penalty for getting a wrong answer. Even if you have no idea about a question, you still have a 20-25% chance of getting it right.

Most test takers do not understand the impact that proper guessing can have on their score. Unless you score extremely high, guessing will significantly contribute to your final score.

Monkeys Take the Test

What most test takers don't realize is that to insure that 20-25% chance, you have to guess randomly. If you put 20 monkeys in a room to take this test, assuming they answered once per question and behaved themselves, on average they would get 20-25% of the questions correct. Put 20 test takers in the room, and the average will be much lower among guessed questions. Why?
1. The test writers intentionally write deceptive answer choices that "look" right. A test taker has no idea about a question, so he picks the "best looking" answer, which is often wrong. The monkey has no idea what looks good and what doesn't, so it will consistently be right about 20-25% of the time.
2. Test takers will eliminate answer choices from the guessing pool based on a hunch or intuition. Simple but correct answers often get excluded, leaving a 0% chance of being correct. The monkey has no clue, and often gets lucky with the best choice.

This is why the process of elimination endorsed by most test courses is flawed and detrimental to your performance. Test takers don't guess; they make an ignorant stab in the dark that is usually worse than random.

$5 Challenge

Let me introduce one of the most valuable ideas of this course—the $5 challenge:

You only mark your "best guess" if you are willing to bet $5 on it.
You only eliminate choices from guessing if you are willing to bet $5 on it.

Why $5? Five dollars is an amount of money that is small yet not insignificant, and can really add up fast (20 questions could cost you $100). Likewise, each answer choice on one question of the test will have a small impact on your overall score, but it can really add up to a lot of points in the end.

The process of elimination IS valuable. The following shows your chance of guessing it right:

If you eliminate wrong answer choices until only this many remain:	Chance of getting it correct:
1	100%
2	50%
3	33%

However, if you accidentally eliminate the right answer or go on a hunch for an incorrect answer, your chances drop dramatically—to 0%. By guessing among all the answer choices, you are GUARANTEED to have a shot at the right answer.

That's why the $5 test is so valuable. If you give up the advantage and safety of a pure guess, it had better be worth the risk.

What we still haven't covered is how to be sure that whatever guess you make is truly random. Here's the easiest way:

Always pick the first answer choice among those remaining.

Such a technique means that you have decided, **before you see a single test question**, exactly how you are going to guess, and since the order of choices tells you nothing about which one is correct, this guessing technique is perfectly random.

This section is not meant to scare you away from making educated guesses or eliminating choices; you just need to define when a choice is worth eliminating. The $5 test, along with a pre-defined random guessing strategy, is the best way to make sure you reap all of the benefits of guessing.

Secret Key #3 - Practice Smarter, Not Harder

Many test takers delay the test preparation process because they dread the awful amounts of practice time they think necessary to succeed on the test. We have refined an effective method that will take you only a fraction of the time.

There are a number of "obstacles" in the path to success. Among these are answering questions, finishing in time, and mastering test-taking strategies. All must be executed on the day of the test at peak performance, or your score will suffer. The test is a mental marathon that has a large impact on your future.

Just like a marathon runner, it is important to work your way up to the full challenge. So first you just worry about questions, and then time, and finally strategy:

Success Strategy

1. Find a good source for practice tests.
2. If you are willing to make a larger time investment, consider using more than one study guide. Often the different approaches of multiple authors will help you "get" difficult concepts.
3. Take a practice test with no time constraints, with all study helps, "open book." Take your time with questions and focus on applying strategies.
4. Take a practice test with time constraints, with all guides, "open book."
5. Take a final practice test without open material and with time limits.

If you have time to take more practice tests, just repeat step 5. By gradually exposing yourself to the full rigors of the test environment, you will condition your mind to the stress of test day and maximize your success.

Secret Key #4 - Prepare, Don't Procrastinate

Let me state an obvious fact: if you take the test three times, you will probably get three different scores. This is due to the way you feel on test day, the level of preparedness you have, and the version of the test you see. Despite the test writers' claims to the contrary, some versions of the test WILL be easier for you than others.

Since your future depends so much on your score, you should maximize your chances of success. In order to maximize the likelihood of success, you've got to prepare in advance. This means taking practice tests and spending time learning the information and test taking strategies you will need to succeed.

Never go take the actual test as a "practice" test, expecting that you can just take it again if you need to. Take all the practice tests you can on your own, but when you go to take the official test, be prepared, be focused, and do your best the first time!

Secret Key #5 - Test Yourself

Everyone knows that time is money. There is no need to spend too much of your time or too little of your time preparing for the test. You should only spend as much of your precious time preparing as is necessary for you to get the score you need.

Once you have taken a practice test under real conditions of time constraints, then you will know if you are ready for the test or not.

If you have scored extremely high the first time that you take the practice test, then there is not much point in spending countless hours studying. You are already there.

Benchmark your abilities by retaking practice tests and seeing how much you have improved. Once you consistently score high enough to guarantee success, then you are ready.

If you have scored well below where you need, then knuckle down and begin studying in earnest. Check your improvement regularly through the use of practice tests under real conditions. Above all, don't worry, panic, or give up. The key is perseverance!

Then, when you go to take the test, remain confident and remember how well you did on the practice tests. If you can score high enough on a practice test, then you can do the same on the real thing.

General Strategies

The most important thing you can do is to ignore your fears and jump into the test immediately. Do not be overwhelmed by any strange-sounding terms. You have to jump into the test like jumping into a pool—all at once is the easiest way.

Make Predictions

As you read and understand the question, try to guess what the answer will be. Remember that several of the answer choices are wrong, and once you begin reading them, your mind will immediately become cluttered with answer choices designed to throw you off. Your mind is typically the most focused immediately after you have read the question and digested its contents. If you can, try to predict what the correct answer will be. You may be surprised at what you can predict.

Quickly scan the choices and see if your prediction is in the listed answer choices. If it is, then you can be quite confident that you have the right answer. It still won't hurt to check the other answer choices, but most of the time, you've got it!

Answer the Question

It may seem obvious to only pick answer choices that answer the question, but the test writers can create some excellent answer choices that are wrong. Don't pick an answer just because it sounds right, or you believe it to be true. It MUST answer the question. Once you've made your selection, always go back and check it against the question and make sure that you didn't misread the question and that the answer choice does answer the question posed.

Benchmark

After you read the first answer choice, decide if you think it sounds correct or not. If it doesn't, move on to the next answer choice. If it does, mentally mark that answer choice. This doesn't mean that you've definitely selected it as your answer choice, it just means that it's the best you've seen thus far. Go ahead and read the next choice. If the next choice is worse than the one you've already selected, keep going to the next answer choice. If the next choice is better than the choice you've already selected, mentally mark the new answer choice as your best guess.

The first answer choice that you select becomes your standard. Every other answer choice must be benchmarked against that standard. That choice is correct until proven otherwise by another answer choice beating it out. Once you've decided that no other answer choice seems as good, do one final check to ensure that your answer choice answers the question posed.

Valid Information

Don't discount any of the information provided in the question. Every piece of information may be necessary to determine the correct answer. None of the information in the question is there to throw you off (while the answer choices will certainly have information to throw you off). If two seemingly unrelated topics are discussed, don't ignore either. You can be confident there is a relationship, or it wouldn't be included in the question, and you are probably going to have to determine what is that relationship to find the answer.

Avoid "Fact Traps"

Don't get distracted by a choice that is factually true. Your search is for the answer that answers the question. Stay focused and don't fall for an answer that is true but irrelevant. Always go back to the question and make sure you're choosing an answer that actually answers the question and is not just a true statement. An answer can be factually correct, but it MUST answer the question asked. Additionally, two answers can both be seemingly correct, so be sure to read all of the answer choices, and make sure that you get the one that BEST answers the question.

Milk the Question

Some of the questions may throw you completely off. They might deal with a subject you have not been exposed to, or one that you haven't reviewed in years. While your lack of knowledge about the subject will be a hindrance, the question itself can give you many clues that will help you find the correct answer. Read the question carefully and look for clues. Watch particularly for adjectives and nouns describing difficult terms or words that you don't recognize. Regardless of whether you completely understand a word or not, replacing it with a synonym, either provided or one you more familiar with, may help you to understand what the questions are asking. Rather than wracking your mind about specific detailed information concerning a difficult term or word, try to use mental substitutes that are easier to understand.

The Trap of Familiarity

Don't just choose a word because you recognize it. On difficult questions, you may not recognize a number of words in the answer choices. The test writers don't put "make-believe" words on the test, so don't think that just because you only recognize all the words in one answer choice that that answer choice must be correct. If you only recognize words in one answer choice, then focus on that one. Is it correct? Try your best to determine if it is correct. If it is, that's great. If not, eliminate it. Each word and answer choice you eliminate increases your chances of getting the question correct, even if you then have to guess among the unfamiliar choices.

Eliminate Answers

Eliminate choices as soon as you realize they are wrong. But be careful! Make sure you consider all of the possible answer choices. Just because one appears right, doesn't mean that the next one won't be even better! The test writers will usually put more than one good answer choice for every question, so read all of them. Don't worry if you are stuck between two that seem right. By getting down to just two remaining possible choices, your odds are now 50/50. Rather than wasting too much time, play the odds. You are guessing, but guessing wisely because you've been able to knock out some of the answer choices that you know are wrong. If you are eliminating choices and realize that the last answer choice you are left with is also obviously wrong, don't panic. Start over and consider each choice again. There may easily be something that you missed the first time and will realize on the second pass.

Tough Questions

If you are stumped on a problem or it appears too hard or too difficult, don't waste time. Move on! Remember though, if you can quickly check for obviously incorrect answer choices, your chances of guessing correctly are greatly improved. Before you completely give up, at least try to knock out a couple of possible answers. Eliminate what you can and then guess at the remaining answer choices before moving on.

Brainstorm

If you get stuck on a difficult question, spend a few seconds quickly brainstorming. Run through the complete list of possible answer choices. Look at each choice and ask yourself, "Could this answer the question satisfactorily?" Go through each answer choice and consider it independently of the others. By systematically going through all possibilities, you may find something that you would otherwise overlook. Remember though that when you get stuck, it's important to try to keep moving.

Read Carefully

Understand the problem. Read the question and answer choices carefully. Don't miss the question because you misread the terms. You have plenty of time to read each question thoroughly and make sure you understand what is being asked. Yet a happy medium must be attained, so don't waste too much time. You must read carefully, but efficiently.

Face Value

When in doubt, use common sense. Always accept the situation in the problem at face value. Don't read too much into it. These problems will not require you to make huge leaps of logic. The test writers aren't trying to throw you off with a cheap trick. If you have to go beyond creativity and make a leap of logic in order to have an answer choice answer the question, then you should look at the other answer choices. Don't overcomplicate the problem by creating theoretical relationships or explanations that will warp time or space. These are normal problems rooted in reality. It's just that the applicable relationship or explanation may not be readily apparent and you have to figure things out. Use your common sense to interpret anything that isn't clear.

Prefixes

If you're having trouble with a word in the question or answer choices, try dissecting it. Take advantage of every clue that the word might include. Prefixes and suffixes can be a huge help. Usually they allow you to determine a basic meaning. Pre- means before, post- means after, pro - is positive, de- is negative. From these prefixes and suffixes, you can get an idea of the general meaning of the word and try to put it into context. Beware though of any traps. Just because con- is the opposite of pro-, doesn't necessarily mean congress is the opposite of progress!

Hedge Phrases

Watch out for critical hedge phrases, led off with words such as "likely," "may," "can," "sometimes," "often," "almost," "mostly," "usually," "generally," "rarely," and "sometimes." Question writers insert these hedge phrases to cover every possibility. Often an answer choice will be wrong simply because it leaves no room for exception. Unless the situation calls for them, avoid answer choices that have definitive words like "exactly," and "always."

Switchback Words

Stay alert for "switchbacks." These are the words and phrases frequently used to alert you to shifts in thought. The most common switchback word is "but." Others include "although," "however," "nevertheless," "on the other hand," "even though," "while," "in spite of," "despite," and "regardless of."

New Information

Correct answer choices will rarely have completely new information included. Answer choices typically are straightforward reflections of the material asked about and will directly relate to the question. If a new piece of information is included in an answer choice that doesn't even seem to relate to the topic being asked about, then that answer choice is likely incorrect. All of the information needed to answer the question is usually provided for you in the question. You should not have to make guesses that are unsupported or choose answer choices that require unknown information that cannot be reasoned from what is given.

Time Management

On technical questions, don't get lost on the technical terms. Don't spend too much time on any one question. If you don't know what a term means, then odds are you aren't going to get much further since you don't have a dictionary. You should be able to immediately recognize whether or not you know a term. If you don't, work with the other clues that you have—the other answer choices and terms provided—but don't waste too much time trying to figure out a difficult term that you don't know.

Contextual Clues

Look for contextual clues. An answer can be right but not the correct answer. The contextual clues will help you find the answer that is most right and is correct. Understand the context in which a phrase or statement is made. This will help you make important distinctions.

Don't Panic

Panicking will not answer any questions for you; therefore, it isn't helpful. When you first see the question, if your mind goes blank, take a deep breath. Force yourself to mechanically go through the steps of solving the problem using the strategies you've learned.

Pace Yourself

Don't get clock fever. It's easy to be overwhelmed when you're looking at a page full of questions, your mind is full of random thoughts and feeling confused, and the clock is ticking down faster than you would like. Calm down and maintain the pace that you have set for yourself. As long as you are on track by monitoring your pace, you are guaranteed to have enough time for yourself. When you get to the last few minutes of the test, it may seem like you won't have enough time left, but if you only have as many questions as you should have left at that point, then you're right on track!

Answer Selection

The best way to pick an answer choice is to eliminate all of those that are wrong, until only one is left and confirm that is the correct answer. Sometimes though, an answer choice may immediately look right. Be careful! Take a second to make sure that the other choices are not equally obvious. Don't make a hasty mistake. There are only two times that you should stop before checking other answers. First is when you are positive that the answer choice you have selected is correct. Second is when time is almost out and you have to make a quick guess!

Check Your Work

Since you will probably not know every term listed and the answer to every question, it is important that you get credit for the ones that you do know. Don't miss any questions through careless mistakes. If at all possible, try to take a second to look back over your answer selection and make sure you've selected the correct answer choice and haven't made a costly careless mistake (such as marking an answer choice that you didn't mean to mark). The time it takes for this quick double check should more than pay for itself in caught mistakes.

Beware of Directly Quoted Answers

Sometimes an answer choice will repeat word for word a portion of the question or reference section. However, beware of such exact duplication. It may be a trap! More than likely, the correct choice will paraphrase or summarize a point, rather than being exactly the same wording.

Slang

Scientific sounding answers are better than slang ones. An answer choice that begins "To compare the outcomes..." is much more likely to be correct than one that begins "Because some people insisted..."

Extreme Statements

Avoid wild answers that throw out highly controversial ideas that are proclaimed as established fact. An answer choice that states the "process should used in certain situations, if…" is much more likely to be correct than one that states the "process should be discontinued completely." The first is a calm rational statement and doesn't even make a definitive, uncompromising stance, using a hedge word "if" to provide wiggle room, whereas the second choice is a radical idea and far more extreme.

Answer Choice Families

When you have two or more answer choices that are direct opposites or parallels, one of them is usually the correct answer. For instance, if one answer choice states "x increases" and another answer choice states "x decreases" or "y increases," then those two or three answer choices are very similar in construction and fall into the same family of answer choices. A family of answer choices consists of two or three answer choices, very similar in construction, but often with directly opposite meanings. Usually the correct answer choice will be in that family of answer choices. The "odd man out" or answer choice that doesn't seem to fit the parallel construction of the other answer choices is more likely to be incorrect.

Special Report: How to Overcome Test Anxiety

The very nature of tests caters to some level of anxiety, nervousness, or tension, just as we feel for any important event that occurs in our lives. A little bit of anxiety or nervousness can be a good thing. It helps us with motivation, and makes achievement just that much sweeter. However, too much anxiety can be a problem, especially if it hinders our ability to function and perform.

"Test anxiety," is the term that refers to the emotional reactions that some test-takers experience when faced with a test or exam. Having a fear of testing and exams is based upon a rational fear, since the test-taker's performance can shape the course of an academic career. Nevertheless, experiencing excessive fear of examinations will only interfere with the test-taker's ability to perform and chance to be successful.

There are a large variety of causes that can contribute to the development and sensation of test anxiety. These include, but are not limited to, lack of preparation and worrying about issues surrounding the test.

Lack of Preparation

Lack of preparation can be identified by the following behaviors or situations:

Not scheduling enough time to study, and therefore cramming the night before the test or exam
Managing time poorly, to create the sensation that there is not enough time to do everything
Failing to organize the text information in advance, so that the study material consists of the entire text and not simply the pertinent information
Poor overall studying habits

Worrying, on the other hand, can be related to both the test taker, or many other factors around him/her that will be affected by the results of the test. These include worrying about:

Previous performances on similar exams, or exams in general
How friends and other students are achieving
The negative consequences that will result from a poor grade or failure

There are three primary elements to test anxiety. Physical components, which involve the same typical bodily reactions as those to acute anxiety (to be discussed below). Emotional factors have to do with fear or panic. Mental or cognitive issues concerning attention spans and memory abilities.

Physical Signals

There are many different symptoms of test anxiety, and these are not limited to mental and emotional strain. Frequently there are a range of physical signals that will let a test taker know that he/she is suffering from test anxiety. These bodily changes can include the following:

Perspiring
Sweaty palms
Wet, trembling hands
Nausea
Dry mouth
A knot in the stomach
Headache
Faintness
Muscle tension
Aching shoulders, back and neck
Rapid heart beat
Feeling too hot/cold

To recognize the sensation of test anxiety, a test-taker should monitor him/herself for the following sensations:

The physical distress symptoms as listed above
Emotional sensitivity, expressing emotional feelings such as the need to cry or laugh too much, or a sensation of anger or helplessness
A decreased ability to think, causing the test-taker to blank out or have racing thoughts that are hard to organize or control.

Though most students will feel some level of anxiety when faced with a test or exam, the majority can cope with that anxiety and maintain it at a manageable level. However, those who cannot are faced with a very real and very serious condition, which can and should be controlled for the immeasurable benefit of this sufferer.

Naturally, these sensations lead to negative results for the testing experience. The most common effects of test anxiety have to do with nervousness and mental blocking.

Nervousness

Nervousness can appear in several different levels:

The test-taker's difficulty, or even inability to read and understand the questions on the test

The difficulty or inability to organize thoughts to a coherent form

The difficulty or inability to recall key words and concepts relating to the testing questions (especially essays)

The receipt of poor grades on a test, though the test material was well known by the test taker

Conversely, a person may also experience mental blocking, which involves:

Blanking out on test questions

Only remembering the correct answers to the questions when the test has already finished.

Fortunately for test anxiety sufferers, beating these feelings, to a large degree, has to do with proper preparation. When a test taker has a feeling of preparedness, then anxiety will be dramatically lessened.

The first step to resolving anxiety issues is to distinguish which of the two types of anxiety are being suffered. If the anxiety is a direct result of a lack of preparation, this should be considered a normal reaction, and the anxiety level (as opposed to the test results) shouldn't be anything to worry about. However, if, when adequately prepared, the test-taker still panics, blanks out, or seems to overreact, this is not a fully rational reaction. While this can be considered normal too, there are many ways to combat and overcome these effects.

Remember that anxiety cannot be entirely eliminated, however, there are ways to minimize it, to make the anxiety easier to manage. Preparation is one of the best ways to minimize test anxiety. Therefore the following techniques are wise in order to best fight off any anxiety that may want to build.

To begin with, try to avoid cramming before a test, whenever it is possible. By trying to memorize an entire term's worth of information in one day, you'll be shocking your system, and not giving yourself a very good chance to absorb the information. This is an easy path to anxiety, so for those who suffer from test anxiety, cramming should not even be considered an option.

Instead of cramming, work throughout the semester to combine all of the material which is presented throughout the semester, and work on it gradually as the course goes by, making sure to master the main concepts first, leaving minor details for a week or so before the test.

To study for the upcoming exam, be sure to pose questions that may be on the examination, to gauge the ability to answer them by integrating the ideas from your texts, notes and lectures, as well as any supplementary readings.

If it is truly impossible to cover all of the information that was covered in that particular term, concentrate on the most important portions, that can be covered very well. Learn these concepts as best as possible, so that when the test comes, a goal can be made to use these concepts as presentations of your knowledge.

In addition to study habits, changes in attitude are critical to beating a struggle with test anxiety. In fact, an improvement of the perspective over the entire test-taking experience can actually help a test taker to enjoy studying and therefore improve the overall experience. Be certain not to overemphasize the significance of the grade - know that the result of the test is neither a reflection of self worth, nor is it a measure of intelligence; one grade will not predict a person's future success.

To improve an overall testing outlook, the following steps should be tried:

Keeping in mind that the most reasonable expectation for taking a test is to expect to try to demonstrate as much of what you know as you possibly can. Reminding ourselves that a test is only one test; this is not the only one, and there will be others.
The thought of thinking of oneself in an irrational, all-or-nothing term should be avoided at all costs.
A reward should be designated for after the test, so there's something to look forward to. Whether it be going to a movie, going out to eat, or simply visiting friends, schedule it in advance, and do it no matter what result is expected on the exam.

Test-takers should also keep in mind that the basics are some of the most important things, even beyond anti-anxiety techniques and studying. Never neglect the basic social, emotional and biological needs, in order to try to absorb information. In order to best achieve, these three factors must be held as just as important as the studying itself.

Study Steps

Remember the following important steps for studying:

Maintain healthy nutrition and exercise habits. Continue both your recreational activities and social pass times. These both contribute to your physical and emotional well being.
Be certain to get a good amount of sleep, especially the night before the test, because when you're overtired you are not able to perform to the best of your best ability.
Keep the studying pace to a moderate level by taking breaks when they are needed, and varying the work whenever possible, to keep the mind fresh instead of getting bored.
When enough studying has been done that all the material that can be learned has been learned, and the test taker is prepared for the test, stop studying and do

something relaxing such as listening to music, watching a movie, or taking a warm bubble bath.

There are also many other techniques to minimize the uneasiness or apprehension that is experienced along with test anxiety before, during, or even after the examination. In fact, there are a great deal of things that can be done to stop anxiety from interfering with lifestyle and performance. Again, remember that anxiety will not be eliminated entirely, and it shouldn't be. Otherwise that "up" feeling for exams would not exist, and most of us depend on that sensation to perform better than usual. However, this anxiety has to be at a level that is manageable.

Of course, as we have just discussed, being prepared for the exam is half the battle right away. Attending all classes, finding out what knowledge will be expected on the exam, and knowing the exam schedules are easy steps to lowering anxiety. Keeping up with work will remove the need to cram, and efficient study habits will eliminate wasted time. Studying should be done in an ideal location for concentration, so that it is simple to become interested in the material and give it complete attention. A method such as SQ3R (Survey, Question, Read, Recite, Review) is a wonderful key to follow to make sure that the study habits are as effective as possible, especially in the case of learning from a textbook. Flashcards are great techniques for memorization. Learning to take good notes will mean that notes will be full of useful information, so that less sifting will need to be done to seek out what is pertinent for studying. Reviewing notes after class and then again on occasion will keep the information fresh in the mind. From notes that have been taken summary sheets and outlines can be made for simpler reviewing.

A study group can also be a very motivational and helpful place to study, as there will be a sharing of ideas, all of the minds can work together, to make sure that everyone understands, and the studying will be made more interesting because it will be a social occasion.

Basically, though, as long as the test-taker remains organized and self confident, with efficient study habits, less time will need to be spent studying, and higher grades will be achieved.

To become self confident, there are many useful steps. The first of these is "self talk." It has been shown through extensive research, that self-talk for students who suffer from test anxiety, should be well monitored, in order to make sure that it contributes to self confidence as opposed to sinking the student. Frequently the self talk of test-anxious students is negative or self-defeating, thinking that everyone else is smarter and faster, that they always mess up, and that if they don't do well, they'll fail the entire course. It is important to decreasing anxiety that awareness is made of self talk. Try writing any negative self thoughts and then disputing them with a positive statement instead. Begin self-encouragement as though it was a friend speaking. Repeat positive statements to help reprogram the mind to believing in successes instead of failures.

Helpful Techniques

Other extremely helpful techniques include:

Self-visualization of doing well and reaching goals
While aiming for an "A" level of understanding, don't try to "overprotect" by setting your expectations lower. This will only convince the mind to stop studying in order to meet the lower expectations.
Don't make comparisons with the results or habits of other students. These are individual factors, and different things work for different people, causing different results.
Strive to become an expert in learning what works well, and what can be done in order to improve. Consider collecting this data in a journal.
Create rewards for after studying instead of doing things before studying that will only turn into avoidance behaviors.
Make a practice of relaxing - by using methods such as progressive relaxation, self-hypnosis, guided imagery, etc - in order to make relaxation an automatic sensation.
Work on creating a state of relaxed concentration so that concentrating will take on the focus of the mind, so that none will be wasted on worrying.
Take good care of the physical self by eating well and getting enough sleep.
Plan in time for exercise and stick to this plan.

Beyond these techniques, there are other methods to be used before, during and after the test that will help the test-taker perform well in addition to overcoming anxiety.

Before the exam comes the academic preparation. This involves establishing a study schedule and beginning at least one week before the actual date of the test. By doing this, the anxiety of not having enough time to study for the test will be automatically eliminated. Moreover, this will make the studying a much more effective experience, ensuring that the learning will be an easier process. This relieves much undue pressure on the test-taker.

Summary sheets, note cards, and flash cards with the main concepts and examples of these main concepts should be prepared in advance of the actual studying time. A topic should never be eliminated from this process. By omitting a topic because it isn't expected to be on the test is only setting up the test-taker for anxiety should it actually appear on the exam. Utilize the course syllabus for laying out the topics that should be studied. Carefully go over the notes that were made in class, paying special attention to any of the issues that the professor took special care to emphasize while lecturing in class. In the textbooks, use the chapter review, or if possible, the chapter tests, to begin your review.

It may even be possible to ask the instructor what information will be covered on the exam, or what the format of the exam will be (for example, multiple choice, essay, free form, true-false). Additionally, see if it is possible to find out how many questions will be on the test. If a review sheet or sample test has been offered by the professor, make good use of it, above anything else, for the preparation for the test. Another great resource for getting to know the examination is reviewing tests from previous semesters. Use these tests to review, and aim to achieve a 100% score on each of the possible topics. With a few exceptions, the goal that you set for yourself is the highest one that you will reach.

Take all of the questions that were assigned as homework, and rework them to any other possible course material. The more problems reworked, the more skill and confidence will form as a result. When forming the solution to a problem, write out each of the steps. Don't simply do head work. By doing as many steps on paper as possible, much clarification and therefore confidence will be formed. Do this with as many homework problems as possible, before checking the answers. By checking the answer after each problem, a reinforcement will exist, that will not be on the exam. Study situations should be as exam-like as possible, to prime the test-taker's system for the experience. By waiting to check the answers at the end, a psychological advantage will be formed, to decrease the stress factor.

Another fantastic reason for not cramming is the avoidance of confusion in concepts, especially when it comes to mathematics. 8-10 hours of study will become one hundred percent more effective if it is spread out over a week or at least several days, instead of doing it all in one sitting. Recognize that the human brain requires time in order to assimilate new material, so frequent breaks and a span of study time over several days will be much more beneficial.

Additionally, don't study right up until the point of the exam. Studying should stop a minimum of one hour before the exam begins. This allows the brain to rest and put things in their proper order. This will also provide the time to become as relaxed as possible when going into the examination room. The test-taker will also have time to eat well and eat sensibly. Know that the brain needs food as much as the rest of the body. With enough food and enough sleep, as well as a relaxed attitude, the body and the mind are primed for success.

Avoid any anxious classmates who are talking about the exam. These students only spread anxiety, and are not worth sharing the anxious sentimentalities.

Before the test also involves creating a positive attitude, so mental preparation should also be a point of concentration. There are many keys to creating a positive attitude. Should fears become rushing in, make a visualization of taking the exam, doing well, and seeing an A written on the paper. Write out a list of affirmations that will bring a feeling of confidence, such as "I am doing well in my English class," "I studied well and know my material," "I enjoy this class." Even if the affirmations aren't believed at first, it sends a positive message to the subconscious which will result in an alteration of the overall belief system, which is the system that creates reality.

If a sensation of panic begins, work with the fear and imagine the very worst! Work through the entire scenario of not passing the test, failing the entire course, and dropping out of school, followed by not getting a job, and pushing a shopping cart through the dark alley where you'll live. This will place things into perspective! Then, practice deep breathing and create a visualization of the opposite situation - achieving an "A" on the exam, passing the entire course, receiving the degree at a graduation ceremony.

On the day of the test, there are many things to be done to ensure the best results, as well as the most calm outlook. The following stages are suggested in order to maximize test-taking potential:

Begin the examination day with a moderate breakfast, and avoid any coffee or beverages with caffeine if the test taker is prone to jitters. Even people who are used to managing caffeine can feel jittery or light-headed when it is taken on a test day.

Attempt to do something that is relaxing before the examination begins. As last minute cramming clouds the mastering of overall concepts, it is better to use this time to create a calming outlook.

Be certain to arrive at the test location well in advance, in order to provide time to select a location that is away from doors, windows and other distractions, as well as giving enough time to relax before the test begins.

Keep away from anxiety generating classmates who will upset the sensation of stability and relaxation that is being attempted before the exam.

Should the waiting period before the exam begins cause anxiety, create a self-distraction by reading a light magazine or something else that is relaxing and simple.

During the exam itself, read the entire exam from beginning to end, and find out how much time should be allotted to each individual problem. Once writing the exam, should more time be taken for a problem, it should be abandoned, in order to begin another problem. If there is time at the end, the unfinished problem can always be returned to and completed.

Read the instructions very carefully - twice - so that unpleasant surprises won't follow during or after the exam has ended.

When writing the exam, pretend that the situation is actually simply the completion of homework within a library, or at home. This will assist in forming a relaxed atmosphere, and will allow the brain extra focus for the complex thinking function.

Begin the exam with all of the questions with which the most confidence is felt. This will build the confidence level regarding the entire exam and will begin a quality momentum. This will also create encouragement for trying the problems where uncertainty resides.

Going with the "gut instinct" is always the way to go when solving a problem. Second guessing should be avoided at all costs. Have confidence in the ability to do well.

For essay questions, create an outline in advance that will keep the mind organized and make certain that all of the points are remembered. For multiple choice, read every answer, even if the correct one has been spotted - a better one may exist.

Continue at a pace that is reasonable and not rushed, in order to be able to work carefully. Provide enough time to go over the answers at the end, to check for small errors that can be corrected.

Should a feeling of panic begin, breathe deeply, and think of the feeling of the body releasing sand through its pores. Visualize a calm, peaceful place, and include all of the sights, sounds and sensations of this image. Continue the deep breathing, and take a few minutes to continue this with closed eyes. When all is well again, return to the test.

If a "blanking" occurs for a certain question, skip it and move on to the next question. There will be time to return to the other question later. Get everything done that can be done, first, to guarantee all the grades that can be compiled, and to build all of the confidence possible. Then return to the weaker questions to build the marks from there.

Remember, one's own reality can be created, so as long as the belief is there, success will follow. And remember: anxiety can happen later, right now, there's an exam to be written!

After the examination is complete, whether there is a feeling for a good grade or a bad grade, don't dwell on the exam, and be certain to follow through on the reward that was promised...and enjoy it! Don't dwell on any mistakes that have been made, as there is nothing that can be done at this point anyway.

Additionally, don't begin to study for the next test right away. Do something relaxing for a while, and let the mind relax and prepare itself to begin absorbing information again.

From the results of the exam - both the grade and the entire experience, be certain to learn from what has gone on. Perfect studying habits and work some more on confidence in order to make the next examination experience even better than the last one.

Learn to avoid places where openings occurred for laziness, procrastination and day dreaming.

Use the time between this exam and the next one to better learn to relax, even learning to relax on cue, so that any anxiety can be controlled during the next exam. Learn how to relax the body. Slouch in your chair if that helps. Tighten and then relax all of the different muscle groups, one group at a time, beginning with the feet and then working all the way up to the neck and face. This will ultimately relax the muscles more than they were to begin with. Learn how to breathe deeply and comfortably, and focus on this breathing going in and out as a relaxing thought. With every exhale, repeat the word "relax."

As common as test anxiety is, it is very possible to overcome it. Make yourself one of the test-takers who overcome this frustrating hindrance.

Additional Bonus Material

Due to our efforts to try to keep this book to a manageable length, we've created a link that will give you access to all of your additional bonus material.

Please visit http://www.mometrix.com/bonus948/cgfm1ge to access the information.